The Military We Need

The Military We Need
The Defense Requirements of the Bush Doctrine

Thomas Donnelly

The AEI Press

Publisher for the American Enterprise Institute

WASHINGTON, D.C.

Available in the United States from the AEI Press, c/o Client Distribution Services, 193 Edwards Drive, Jackson, TN 38301. To order, call toll free: 1-800-343-4499. Distributed outside the United States by arrangement with Eurospan, 3 Henrietta Street, London WC2E 8LU, England.

Library of Congress Cataloging-in-Publication Data
Donnelly, Thomas
    The military we need: The defense requirements of the Bush doctrine / Thomas Donnelly.
        p. cm.
    Includes bibliographical references.
    ISBN 0-8447-4229-5 (pbk. : alk. paper)
    1. United States—Armed Forces. 2. United States—Military policy 3. United States—Foreign relations—2001– 4. War on Terrorism, 2001– I. Title.

    UA23.D623 2005
    355'.033573—dc22

                                                    2005007447

10 09 08 07 06 05   1 2 3 4 5 6 7

Cover photograph caption: Members of the U.S. Army 2nd Brigade Combat Team of the 82nd Airborne walk in formation after getting off of the C-5 aircraft (rear) that flew them home from Iraq. The troops had been in Iraq since their deployment in February of 2003.

Printed in the United States of America

Contents

Introduction

The gap between America's strategic reach and its military grasp has reached a point of crisis. It is the task of the second Bush administration to close this gap, but the work transcends party or political ideology. Indeed, it is inherent to the preservation of America's position as global superpower and the great-power peace and broadening prosperity that has marked the post–Cold War era. It is a matter of securing the safety not only of Americans but also of America's friends and allies around the world. And so what otherwise might be mistaken as a piece of bureaucratic busywork by the Pentagon—the 2005 Quadrennial Defense Review (QDR)—becomes crucially important.

Closing the gap between military means and strategic ends is a task that previous defense reviews have failed to carry out. One could argue that, in fact, many of them actually helped to create the gap. Since the collapse of the Soviet Empire, the Department of Defense has conducted three major reviews: the Bottom-Up Review of 1993 and the QDRs of 1997 and 2001. Reviews outside the Pentagon have included the National Defense Panel, meant to provide an independent assessment of the 1997 defense review, and commissions on the roles and missions of the armed forces and the broader national security challenges of the twenty-first century—among the most notable, the so-called Hart-Rudman Commission in 2001 and the September 11 Commission in 2004. There have been at least as many private studies, including one by this author, *Rebuilding America's Defenses: Strategy, Forces and Resources for a New Century*, published in September 2000.

Yet none of these studies fully forecast the strategic and military realities of our post–September 11 world. Most warned of the rising dangers of catastrophic terrorism, but few had the temerity to envision a global war against it, much less a "generational commitment," as Secretary of State Condoleezza Rice has put it, to "transform" the many weak and despotic governments of the greater Middle East into functional democracies.[1] Almost none recommended the military invasions of Afghanistan or Iraq.

Those who warned of a growing great-power challenge from the People's Republic of China (PRC) did not contemplate the containment of Beijing within the context of a global war on terrorism. The security of South Asia was viewed predominantly through the lens of nuclear nonproliferation. And Africa was viewed, when viewed at all, entirely as a humanitarian or epidemiological problem, hardly a matter for normal policy or strategy making.

To be fair, none of these previous studies, including the 2001 QDR, had the benefit of the guidance of the Bush Doctrine, as expressed in *The National Security Strategy of the United States*, released by the White House in September 2002.[2] Although the Bush Doctrine is best understood as a set of strategic goals for the United States in a post–September 11 world, rather than a coherent how-to approach to achieving them, it does provide a benchmark for Pentagon planners.[3] Most important, it establishes the greater Middle East as a central strategic concern and advocates fundamental political change in the region. It moves the Middle East to center stage of American foreign policy and demands long-term strategic engagement, rather than a limited or periodic commitment. An explication of these strategic goals is essential for attempting to answer the central question of any defense program: How much is enough? Recent defense reviews have had to assume—or to manipulate—the strategic ends while judging the necessary military means. They were castles built on air.

In some ways, the sharpest ends-means dichotomy is between the Bush Doctrine of 2005 and the Bush administration's 2001 defense review. Though the QDR was published not long before *National Security Strategy*, they were spawned in vastly different geopolitical eras. The attacks of 9/11 marked a sharp break in Bush administration thinking and brought the president himself to center stage in strategy making. The wars in Afghanistan and Iraq have sharpened the break: no longer is there talk of a decades-long "strategic pause" during which the United States could ready itself for the rise of China or some other great power or coalition of great powers. Constabulary, nation-building missions no longer seem the feckless squandering of U.S. troop strength through Clinton-era international "social work" but rather the key in determining whether the U.S. invasions of Iraq and Afghanistan will end in victory or defeat.[4] Transforming the military to be a swifter, more efficient firepower machine seems secondary to transforming the force to execute enduring, manpower-intensive missions patrolling the American security perimeter. Indeed, had the course plotted in the 2001 QDR been pursued more fully, the United States might have been even less prepared for the post-9/11 world, particularly for the reconstruction of Iraq and Afghanistan and the broader mission of transforming the Middle East.

In recent months, the Bush administration has come to entertain the possibility that there might be shortcomings in the planning assumptions embedded in its defense program. Yet, to the extent the formal *National Military Strategy* reflects the state of current Defense Department thinking, there is still great reluctance to face up to the full consequences of the president's vision.

In the Pentagon, a debate persists over the current level of U.S. commitment to the Middle East. The hope is that large-scale operations in Iraq, Afghanistan, and elsewhere in the region represent a temporary spike in activity, not the new baseline of engagement. Although Defense Secretary Donald Rumsfeld has retreated from his initial position against increasing the strength of the active-duty army, he resists taking any formal, legislative steps to increase its size permanently.

Thus, the two formal Pentagon strategy documents, Rumsfeld's 2005 *National Defense Strategy* and Chairman of the

Joint Chiefs of Staff General Richard Myers's complementary 2004 *National Military Strategy*, retain the 2001 QDR's "1-4-2-1" force-sizing construct. The "1-4-2-1" construct directs "a force sized to defend the homeland, deter [enemies] . . . in and from four regions, and conduct two, overlapping 'swift defeat' campaigns." Furthermore—and most crucial—"the force must be able to 'win decisively' in one of these two campaigns."[5] Simply put, despite the experience of Afghanistan and Iraq, the Pentagon leadership does not believe it necessary to alter its fundamental strategy or force-sizing construct.

The events of the past two years, and particularly the extended counterinsurgency campaign in Iraq, reveal how bankrupt this thinking is. Operation Iraqi Freedom began as a "swift defeat" campaign—and, notably, achieved its regime-removal purpose with a smaller force than planned, while the Fourth Infantry Division was still mostly in transit from Turkey to Kuwait. But it turns out that winning decisively in Iraq—enough to permit a return of sovereignty, democratic elections, and a modicum of security—is a tougher task and a longer obligation than Pentagon planners imagined. Moreover, even if the United States successfully accomplishes these immediate goals, it will remain obligated to help a free Iraq defend itself in a hostile region. There is a substantial "deter forward" mission that looms after the "win decisively" work is done. And what is true in Iraq is also true on a smaller scale in Afghanistan.

Even as the demands of these fairly well-delineated missions are increasing, the new military strategy fails to acknowledge them in its "baseline security posture": the U.S. regional commands are now to regard the activities of the global war on terrorism as part of their normal, day-to-day duties. Even if we set aside Iraq and Afghanistan, the range of these activities over the past two years has been substantial and staggeringly disparate. Since the September 11 attacks, operations have extended from the jungles of the Philippines to the mountains of Georgia to the wastelands of the southern Sahara. As the strategy admits:

> The extremely demanding circumstances associated with the ongoing [war on terrorism] are likely to endure for the foreseeable future. Because post-conflict and [war on terrorism] operations are likely of long duration and will vary in intensity, planners must account for the capabilities required to achieve campaign objectives.[6]

Another shortcoming of the strategy's force-sizing construct is its fantasy of disengagement. It is worth recalling that the Bush administration came to power ridiculing its predecessor's commitment to the Balkans. Although most U.S. troops have departed Bosnia-Herzegovina, having ceded responsibility for that country to the European Union, NATO is still engaged on the ground in Kosovo with more than 17,000 troops, whose presence remains crucial to preventing the resurgence of Serb-Albanian violence. U.S. commitments to the Middle East must be similarly long lasting.

Finally, the Pentagon does seem to have realized that there are opportunity costs to its project of "force transformation."[7] Far from being a cheap solution for military effectiveness, transformation is, essentially, an additional mission for a smaller force— at times, furthermore, a voluntary mission that runs directly contrary to the other missions we have.

It is the job of the new administration to begin at last to close the gap between strategic ends and military means. President Bush has articulated a bold new vision of the world the United States should build; one can only describe it as a genuinely liberal strategy, appealing to that most American of human instincts: the desire for freedom. The purpose of this paper is to suggest how to measure the success of the 2005 QDR, elaborating a strategy appropriate to the goals of the Bush Doctrine, defining the military missions inherent in such a strategy, describing the military institutions needed to execute those missions, and discussing the budgets necessary to build and sustain the institutions. No single scholar can hope to replicate the depth and detail of analysis available to the Defense Department. This is, therefore, not a "shadow" defense review. Rather, it is a paper about how to think about the 2005 QDR and the challenges our military must confront in a post-9/11 world.

1

Strategies

As the Cold War progressed, the American ability to think strategically seemed to atrophy. After the denouement of the Cuban Missile Crisis, Defense Secretary Robert McNamara famously proclaimed that, in the nuclear age, strategy making had been reduced to crisis management. That statement not only captured the myopia of the Kennedy administration and many of its successors but also reflected their forgetfulness that their predecessors, and particularly the administration of Harry S Truman, had indeed made the strategy of containment almost from whole cloth in response to the aggressive Soviet policies of the late 1940s.

The collapse of the Soviet Union deprived U.S. strategists of a yardstick by which to measure their efforts. Even the best attempts of the immediate post–Cold War years were essentially self-referential. This new era of "Pax Americana"—an era of the sole superpower—was understood to be undoubtedly a good thing, a precious dividend from the long, hard struggle against communism that left free-market democracy as the only viable ideology in an age of globalization. Consequently, the Clinton administration acted as though the Pax Americana would simply "enlarge" itself, requiring only modest efforts to "engage" with the rest of the world, in the words of National Security Adviser Anthony Lake.[1] Thus, the three tasks of the last Clinton-era *National Security Strategy,* published in 1999—"to enhance America's security; to bolster America's economic prosperity; to promote democracy and human rights abroad"—all presume peace.[2]

By contrast, we now believe ourselves to be in the post-9/11 world—a strategic environment that is defined by the reality of conflict. The attacks of September 11, 2001, reminded Americans that some parts of the world revile American hegemony and consider Americans to be their enemies, regardless of what we ourselves may think. Thus, in marked contrast to the Clinton approach, the preface of the Bush administration's 2002 *National Security Strategy* states clearly that America's core objectives are to "defend the peace by fighting terrorists and tyrants, . . . preserve the peace by building good relations among the great powers, . . . [and] extend the peace by encouraging free and open societies on every continent."[3] Peace, in other words, cannot be taken for granted.

Yet at the same time that American perceptions of the world have shifted, the current state of international politics remains in many ways an extension of the previous, post–Cold War environment insofar as the fundamental correlation of power in the world remains the same. The new century is still a moment of unprecedented great-power peace. The former great powers of Europe, in addition to being far less great, are peaceful almost to the point of pacifism, as is Japan. One rising great power, India, is already a thriving democracy, and its pressing security problems of terrorism and the nuclear balance with Pakistan are not immediately the stuff of world wars. China's rise is potentially the most destabilizing change in the future, and its immediate threat to Taiwan carries within it the danger of disrupting the current great-power peace. Yet by any historical standard, the danger of global conflict among wealthy nations is at an all-time low.

Moreover, this very stable international order is amazingly liberal. The world is not only enjoying a moment of remarkable peace but also experiencing an even more amazing moment of human liberty. The "captive nations" of Eastern Europe are free. Genuinely liberal democracies, with protections for minorities, the rule of law, property rights, and even reasonably transparent governments, are flourishing in cultures previously believed to be inhospitable to these supposedly Western values. And the Bush administration has ensured that, though fraught with challenges and no means assured in its outcome, any dialogue about the future of the greater Middle East will also be a dialogue about democracy and fundamental human rights for the inhabitants of that region, whose oppression and disenfranchisement were previously impolitic topics for American administrations.

With headlines and newscasts dominated by violence, it is easy to lose sight of these larger facts. And it is even more diffcult to remind ourselves what links these two historically unprecedented moments of peace and liberty. They are the product of an equally unique fact: the global preeminence of a single liberal state, a sole superpower, the United States of America. The post-9/11 security environment is still, unmistakably, the era of Pax Americana.

National Security Strategy

It remains to be seen whether the United States has the will and the wherewithal to maintain the Pax Americana. Although the collapse of the Soviet Union placed us in a quasi-imperial role, that was hardly our goal in the Cold War. Indeed, for several decades, American policymakers considered peaceful coexistence with Moscow the best strategic goal toward which Washington could reasonably strive. In the choice between domestic entitlements at home and open-ended security commitments abroad, might the American people prefer to shed their superpower status?

Despite much national lip biting and soul searching, it is almost impossible to explain the international behavior of the United States over the past fifteen years without concluding that Americans have grown progressively more comfortable— and assured—in their hegemony. It was, after all, the Clinton administration that provoked the French to complain about U.S. *hyperpuissance*, and the 1990s were in fact a time of growing strategic commitments, particularly in the Balkans, as well as traditional commitments kept in the Middle East and East Asia. An expanding security perimeter is a consistent element in American strategic culture, that combination of principles and interests that has defined the historical exercise of power by the United States.

Expansionism not only describes our behavior but also reflects the moral framework through which Americans view the world. Yes, it suited our material interests to prevent a pipsqueak dictator such as Slobodan Milosevic from violating the hard-won peace of Europe, but partition of Bosnia or Serbia would also have suited those interests; ultimately, it was the imperative of American principles, rather than American material interests, that stopped the Balkan slaughter. And likewise, although it is in our strategic interest to build genuine stability in the greater Middle East on the basis of democratic self-governance, the moral argument against the status quo in this region is equally galvanizing.

If we wish to preserve American preeminence, U.S. policymakers must learn the logic of global power in the twenty-first century. The United States needs to maintain both its leadership within the international state structure as well as the legitimacy—moral and practical—of the structure itself. In short, there is a "systemic" or "institutional" dimension to the job of being the sole superpower. Preserving leadership among states is the timeless task of traditional geopolitics. Statesmen have long grasped that the developed states of Europe and East Asia are the elements of great-power politics and that the energy resources of the Middle East are key to industrial economies. Maintaining a favorable disposition of power in these three regions is essential to preserving the global security order.

Yet today the states system of international politics is under increasing pressure. This is most apparent and most immediately threatening in the greater Middle East, where the traditional order is breaking down. Terrorist groups have exploited the weaknesses of central governments in a variety of ways, but the greatest source of their strength is the illegitimacy of these autocratic rulers. But terrorists are hardly the only "non-state actors" dissatisfied with the governance of failing states; pressures from criminal organizations, international businesses, and nongovernmental organizations all undercut the sovereignty of the weak or illegitimate state.

The United States has an interest in maintaining the health and legitimacy of this system, the framework for American power and principles. One task is practical: to strengthen sovereignty in face of problems of failing states and nonstate actors. The second is moral: to strengthen the legitimacy of weak and failing states by bolstering individual political rights, protection of minorities, and the other elements of good governance—"life, liberty, and the pursuit of happiness" writ global.

Challenges to the Pax Americana. Although America's strength and the collapse of the Soviet Union have created a global great-power peace, life under the Pax Americana is hardly without danger. Indeed, some of the most worrisome trends in international politics flow largely from the success of past American policies.

One of the inescapable lessons of the Iraq war is that Europe is now a source of weakness and vulnerability in the liberal international order. The continent is free and at peace, a blessing of historic proportions. (As one contemplates the challenge of transforming the Middle East from the apparently implacable cycle of violence into which it has sunk, it is worth remembering that peaceful, democratic Europe was anything but for most of its history.) And even as Europe slowly aggregates its economic and diplomatic strength through the European Union, the weaknesses of the continent's traditional great powers become more debilitating, not less.

This is a twofold problem of both political will and military strength. European politics are focused inward and are almost completely self-referential; collectively, Europe is nearly irrelevant to the great issues of the future in the Middle East and East Asia. Europe's militaries—and its attempts to forge a collective military—show meager signs of reform. Of the 2.5 million personnel under arms in Europe, only 3 to 5 percent can be deployed, even for a short period.[4] And France and Germany, under the intense fiscal problems caused by poor economic growth, aging populations, and huge welfare burdens, are actually reducing their defense spending. At the same time, they have yet to make any serious reforms in their force structure or defense industry.

At a time when traditional U.S. great-power allies are becoming ever weaker, the People's Republic of China increasingly acts like a great power determined to make its mark on international politics. Beijing has studied the recent operations of the U.S. military intensely, noting both American strengths and weaknesses. China is using its expanding economy to slowly shape its own armed services into a power-projection force; the trend in China is exactly opposite that in Europe. Where this process will lead or end is unknowable, but two facts are clear. First, in local scenarios (and most crucially across the Taiwan Strait), Chinese capabilities already make it difficult for the United States to control any crisis. Second, in the longer term, China is discovering that its regional ambitions are, in a globalized world, inseparable from the larger international security situation. Accommodating China within the context of today's Pax Americana may not be easy.

A rising China poses more of a long-term challenge than the collapse of the traditional order in the greater Middle East, but the latter is the more immediate danger. This unraveling has been under way for some time, accelerating at breakneck speed since the multiple crises of 1979—the pivotal year when the shah fell in Iran, the Soviets invaded Afghanistan, Islamist radicals attempted to seize control of the Grand Mosque in Mecca, and Saddam Hussein openly came to power in Iraq.[5] The rise of radical political Islam, in the form of al Qaeda and its affiliates, is its most spectacular manifestation, spreading from the Arab heartland to the periphery of the Islamic world. There can be no doubt that the status quo in the greater Middle East is the central challenge in international security today, one the United States can no longer ignore. Attacking terrorist groups directly is a necessary but insufficient response to the larger problem, a treatment of the symptoms, not the disease.

Another concern is posed by nuclear or near-nuclear spoiler states, including not only rogue regimes such as North Korea and

Iran but also the governments of Pakistan and Russia, whose control over their doomsday arsenals is questionable. The foremost danger of such states is the possibility that they might transfer nuclear materials to terrorist groups, whether intentionally or inadvertently, through rogue or criminal actors within the regime. Regardless, these states' possession of nuclear weapons severely constrains U.S. policy options for engaging with them. In the case of Iran and Pakistan there are almost no small-scale, "surgical" military operations that do not create more problems than they solve; in the case of Pakistan and Russia, the notion of military operations—even in the aftermath of a nuclear event traced back to their military-industrial complexes—is difficult to fathom.

A final danger, and one given too little thought by U.S. strategy makers, is the possibility that various anti-American actors might make an alliance of convenience. These might be more traditional, state-to-state agreements—China's deepening economic-strategic relationship with Iran occasionally takes on this quality. But such coalitions of the unwilling might easily include nonstate actors such as al Qaeda; indeed, Osama bin Laden's offer of truce to European nations after the March 2004 bombings in Madrid reveals how statelike and political al Qaeda's strategic agenda is. Such agreements would be true axes of evil, even if their strategic cooperation were limited.

The task for the United States is the preservation—and the expansion—of today's Pax Americana, the extension of the "unipolar moment" for as long as possible. The first key to success is to expand and deepen the process of political liberalization in the Islamic world, on the periphery as well as in the Arab heartland. Just as important, however, will be integrating China within the liberal international order—and there is good reason to aspire to this goal, even though it all but implies some form of regime change in Beijing. As *National Security Strategy* warns, "China is following an outdated path that, in the end, will hamper its own pursuit of national greatness. In time, China will find that social and political freedom is the only source of that greatness."[6] Finally, we must preserve the political legitimacy of state structures, as discussed above, by bolstering weak and failing states (including in Europe), constraining the power of even "benign" nonstate actors, and attacking violent nonstate actors.

Setting Strategic Priorities. The first principle of our strategy making is ideological: elaborating President Bush's "forward strategy of freedom" is at the core of the exercise of American power in the world today.[7] This matters internally: that is, the United States must maintain the political will to endure what Defense Secretary Rumsfeld described as the "long, hard slog" in the greater Middle East and simultaneously to engage China diplomatically, economically, and culturally while containing its growing military power.[8] But it matters externally as well: America's political principles are the most powerful aspect of what is now called "soft power," that is, the ability to attract others around the world, both to retain allies and to win over potential enemies. The retreat to realpolitik would be to forgo our most effective strategic tool.

The most pressing of the many separate problems facing the United States come from the greater Middle East, not simply because of the imminent threat of terrorism per se, but because radical Islamism is accelerating the collapse of the traditional order of the region; the states that have been the bulwarks of U.S. strategy are clearly no longer able to provide stability, let alone any true legitimacy. The conventional wisdom is that, after Afghanistan and Iraq, there must be a strategic pause in the process of transforming the region's political order, but that is a matter of faith more than analysis. The region's problems are first and foremost internal problems, which the U.S. military has little role in solving. A provocation by Iran or a crisis in Pakistan, however, might force an American president to respond in ways that require a significant and long-term commitment.

Making progress in the Middle East is also essential to accomplishing the other great task necessary for preserving the Pax Americana: integrating China into the current international order. The "problem of China" is a global challenge. Although the modernizing People's Liberation Army poses a clear and growing threat to Taiwan and to the outdated American strategy of bilateral alliances in East Asia, China, like other industrialized nations, is increasingly dependent on imported energy from the Muslim world. In the material sense, this is of far greater strategic importance to China's great-power aspirations than asserting its claims to Taiwan or, say, in the Spratly Islands. It is also a potential source of grave tension, as China pursues its strategic-economic interests with scarce concern for democratization, good governance, or human rights—thus undermining the lynchpin of America's strategy for the greater Middle East.

In its burgeoning trade with Iran and oil investments in Sudan, China's engagement with the greater Middle East raises the specter of a genuine "axis of evil"—that is, the kind of direct or indirect strategic cooperation among our enemies. We have preserved the Pax Americana to date in part because we have been able to deal with our enemies individually—to divide and conquer, so to speak. Although this is important to our adversaries in the Middle East, where the problems we confront are many but perhaps individually manageable, it is essential in regard to China. Beijing's indication that it will shield Tehran at the UN Security Council from sanctions over its nuclear program, much as it has protected Khartoum from effective action against the genocide in Darfur, may foreshadow the kind of challenge that lies ahead.

A final directive for American strategy makers is initiating some effort to prevent the phenomenon of "democratic weakness" from expanding beyond Western Europe. French and German truculence over Iraq may have had little effect on the battlefield or during reconstruction, but the still greater danger is that such attitudes will spread. But for Tony Blair, who can say what the United Kingdom's policy might have been? To what degree did European pressure influence Turkey's decision not to allow deployment of U.S. forces? The crush of events after 9/11 may have made a larger effort at public diplomacy or military assistance impossible—and some element of European public opinion is beyond the reach of either material or moral appeal—but it is clear that the solidarity of the West is not what it was during the Cold War.

No Real Alternative. American strategists, even as they try to preserve the Pax Americana, would do well to contemplate alternative systems of international security; maintaining the U.S. position as global hegemon, however benignly, could ultimately prove beyond our capacity or our will. If that proves the case, then American policy must be trimmed either by limiting our strategic ends, hoping that means other than military power can achieve the same strategic ends, or by crafting alternative strategies.

For instance, it is possible the United States will face increasing pressure to choose between addressing the problems of the Islamic world and the military containment of China. It may be that multiple, open-ended, and expansive missions in the greater Middle East gradually diffuse U.S. military power, unbalancing the mix of forces to the point where a response to Chinese provocations would be increasingly difficult. Just as Vietnam diverted and warped American military power in the 1960s and 1970s, so might long-term commitments to Afghanistan, Iraq, or other trouble spots distort the global posture of U.S. forces in the future. Conversely, concentrating too much on China or other firepower-intensive scenarios—the preferred choice of many military and civilian leaders in the Defense Department, who still resist the sort of constabulary missions that have become the steady diet of U.S. forces over the past decade—has already left today's force structure unbalanced. In either case, sharing power with China or adopting a more realist approach to the greater Middle East would place the liberal and democratic political foundations of the Pax Americana at risk.

More illusory is the idea that we can have the international system we prefer, but on the cheap. These are the hopes of the soft-power advocates who have dominated the strategic thinking of the Democratic Party since the end of the Cold War and indeed during the late Cold War. A thoroughgoing analysis of soft power is beyond the scope of this paper, but its ability to influence America's enemies is limited, at best, and is more likely to be read as plain weakness in Beijing or in Osama bin Laden's inner councils.

Any alternative strategies would still have to deal with the fact that the collapse of the traditional order in the Middle East is a pressing problem. U.S. strategists have flirted with a form of limited strategic partnership with China; in theory, Beijing has as much interest as the rest of the industrialized world in defeating al Qaeda and keeping the oil flowing. But in practice, China's alleged contributions to the global war on terrorism have consisted mostly of a repressive approach to its own Muslim population, a tactic that is more likely to fuel Islamist radicalism than quell it. Furthermore, as discussed above, China's pursuit of its geostrategic interests in the Islamic world has thus far proved to be more competitive than complementary to American objectives there.

The trouble with such alternatives is that they would shortchange both American principles and interests. This is sometimes necessary, to be sure—the practice of statecraft and strategy demand it—but it is equally important not to confuse tactics with genuine strategy. How the second Bush administration fleshes out the Bush Doctrine—making a genuine strategy out of a broad statement of strategic goals—will go a long way toward determining the shape, extent, and durability of the Pax Americana that has been the framework for general peace and prosperity since the fall of the Berlin Wall.

Military Strategy

A military strategy appropriate to such grand strategic ends will likewise be an ambitious undertaking. The two central tasks—securing the political liberalization of the greater Middle East and offsetting China's growing military and economic strength—are each tall orders in themselves, at once distinct and interwoven, as discussed above. And they call for different kinds of forces.

Achieving these strategic goals demands an explicit "two-theater" strategy—an approach that has been at the core of the American military tradition. Since before the founding, we have always looked outward, in many directions. (Ironically, Americans share a similar strategic perspective with the Chinese in this regard, as we have always viewed the United States as a kind of "Middle Kingdom," a center with security concerns all along its perimeter.) Today, of course, these concerns extend well beyond the colonial frontier and the Americas, past Europe, past the islands of the western Pacific to the Eurasian heartland—quite literally, to the farthest side of the world.

At the same time, the United States has never fully embraced (or provided the resources for) a two-front military capability; there has most often been an element of "swing force" intended to be shifted to the point of decision. Thus, the Panama Canal was essential to permitting a true two-ocean navy, allowing ships to move between the Atlantic and Pacific fleets in a timely fashion. In World War II, Roosevelt agreed to a "Germany first" strategy, and, although both successes and setbacks against Japan complicated this seeming clarity, forces that had fought in Germany were en route for an invasion of the home islands when Tokyo surrendered. Likewise, during the Cold War, forces stationed in the United States might be sent east or west as the situation demanded. Units deployed to fight the Soviets on the central German plain were also counted on to rebuff a North Korean invasion.

The central value of such a military strategy is to permit active engagement and patrolling of the American security perimeter while retaining an operational reserve capable of providing decisive force should a crisis exceed the capacity of forward operating units. This operational reserve also allows for the rotation of personnel in these patrolling missions, ensuring the viability of the forward line of defense over time. Reestablishing this essentially American military strategy is the key to achieving U.S. security goals in the twenty-first century.

Yet recent defense reviews have assumed that setting the size of the force is not strategy, as have Pentagon leaders, even as the unanticipated commitment of forces to Iraq constrains U.S. strategy globally, to the point of disrupting efforts to transform the force or train it. In such long-running struggles as the Cold War or the current effort to reorder the greater Middle East, the size of the force is an essential element in strategy making. The United States needs to maintain a balance of forward operating forces, operational reserves capable of deploying rapidly to points of crisis or relieving forward operating units, and a genuine strategic reserve available in a timely fashion in the event of multiple, large-scale conflicts—in other words, a genuine two-war capability.

Military Strategy to Transform the Greater Middle East. As suggested above, a proper understanding of the greater Middle East reveals a theater of operations of immense size and political and military complexity. In the coming years it is sure to produce multiple U.S. military operations on disparate fronts. Yet just as the region's problems demand an integrated grand strategy, so do they demand a coherent military approach. Realizing a military strategy for the Islamic world will certainly take years, if not decades, and will as often as not be driven by exogenous events rather than conscious American design. Nevertheless, the need for some initial blueprint is desperate—we must try to imagine how we would prefer to prosecute this war.

The primary directive for U.S. military strategy in the greater Middle East should be to retain the initiative won since September 11 through the campaigns in Afghanistan and Iraq. Although the task of transforming the political culture of the Islamic world will inevitably be a long-term effort, the United States must strive to keep our adversaries on the strategic defensive. Individually, the autocratic states and terrorist groups of the region remain relatively weak and susceptible to a divide-and-conquer strategy. Moreover, they do not enjoy any broad great-power support—at least not yet. For the moment, no outside actor is willing to do more than scold the United States for its ambitions in the region. Inaction, in this case, is close enough to consent.

The very weakness of terrorists and the increasingly dispersed nature of their operations give them an elusive, mercurial quality and allow them to reconstitute rapidly when defeated tactically. The foremost object of U.S. strategy must be to deny sanctuary to terrorist groups for the simple reason that, as the 9/11 Commission observed, "a complex international terrorist operation aimed at launching a catastrophic attack cannot be mounted by just anyone in anyplace." Such operations require:

- a time, space, and ability to perform competent planning and staff work;

- a command structure able to make necessary decisions and possessing the authority and contacts to assemble needed people, money, and materials;

- opportunity and space to recruit, train, and select operatives with the needed skills and dedication, providing the time and structure required to socialize them into the terrorist cause, judge their trustworthiness, and hone their skills;

- a logistics network able to securely manage the travel of operatives, move money, and transport resources (like explosives) where they need to go;

- access, in the case of certain weapons, to the special materials needed for a nuclear, chemical, biological, or radiological attack;

- reliable communications between coordinators and operatives; and

- opportunity to test the workability of the plan.[9]

The need for sanctuaries reveals without question that combating al Qaeda–style terrorist groups requires a strategy that also addresses the problems of the larger, state-centered political order in the greater Middle East; they are inseparably interwoven. But for the political peculiarities of the region—both its strengths, such as the wealth its oil reserves have brought, and its weaknesses, such as the corruption and illegitimacy of its governments—the terrorist phenomenon would not be possible or would take a different and less dangerous form.

The greater Middle East abounds with potential sanctuaries for terrorist groups. After the fall of the Taliban from power in Afghanistan, remnants of al Qaeda and affiliated groups have availed themselves of the traditional trade routes and lines of communication throughout the Islamic world, west from Central and South Asia and Arabia into Africa and eastward to Southeast Asia. These paths are also followed by itinerant Wahhabi-style clerics, who proselytize their extreme religious beliefs and accompanying violent politics. These many potential sanctuaries "combine rugged terrain, weak governance, room to hide or receive supplies, and low population density with a town or city near enough to allow necessary interaction with the outside world."[10] These are spread throughout the greater Middle East, as discussed above, including:

- western Pakistan and the Pakistan-Afghanistan border region;

- southern or western Afghanistan;

- the Arabian peninsula, especially Saudi Arabia and Yemen, and the nearby Horn of Africa, extending into Sudan, Somalia, and Kenya;

- Southeast Asia, from Thailand to the southern Philippines to Indonesia;

- West Africa, including Nigeria and Mali;

- North Africa, including the southern Sahara; and

- European cities with expatriate Muslim communities, especially cities in central and eastern Europe where governments are fighting to modernize and reform, and security forces and border controls are less effective.[11]

The scope of military operations throughout the greater Middle East thus has the potential to be immense. Denying the use of any one sanctuary may require relatively little force, yet patrolling and operating across such a vast space will necessarily diffuse and absorb U.S. military strength. As the 9/11 Commission concludes: "In the twentieth century, strategists focused on the world's great industrial heartlands. In the twenty-first, the focus is in the opposite direction, toward remote regions and failing states. The United States has had to find ways to extend its reach, straining the limits of its influence."[12]

Across the region there are a number of states whose combination of weakness and strength makes them vitally important to any coherent U.S. policy; Nigeria, Sudan, Egypt, Saudi Arabia, Iraq, Iran, Afghanistan, Pakistan, Indonesia, and the Philippines would top any list. There is no doubt that assembling these many pieces in a strategic puzzle will be a challenge. Indeed, at any one moment and for many moments to come, several of these states may seem on the verge of crisis.

At the same time, these uncertainties represent strategic opportunities, either to improve the legitimacy and governance of states whose weakness is the danger or to attack terrorist groups directly. In many cases—Morocco or Jordan, for example—both may be possible. In other cases, it may be necessary to prioritize one objective. In Uzbekistan, for instance, the United States should seek to promote democratization at the expense of strategic cooperation with the Karimov regime.

Engagement across the Middle East will, of course, involve other elements of American power, particularly intelligence gathering, but must also include some level of military engagement. In some instances, such as in Nigeria, the goal will be to reform the military, make it responsive to civilian control and a symbol of government legitimacy, while at the same time improving its ability to conduct stability operations and joint operations with U.S. forces. These are very much the traditional tools to "shape" the security environment, but applied in places that have largely been ignored by American strategists in the past.

As much as possible, U.S. strategy for the greater Middle East should strive to balance concerns with the "Arab" heartland (including the non-Arab states of Iran, Afghanistan, and Pakistan)—where the region's problems are most pronounced and most deeply rooted—with the periphery of the Islamic world, where radical Islam is still a weaker force and local cultures are more tolerant. By invading Afghanistan and Iraq, the Bush administration has attacked the problem with characteristic American directness, eliminating al Qaeda's haven and training base and then going to the center of Islamic discontent. In such places as Morocco and Indonesia, however, the costs of engagement are significantly lower, and the potential strategic rewards are great. Not only is it crucial to deny sanctuary to terrorists in such places, but it will also be significantly easier for the United States to partner with local actors in trying to promote democracy, economic growth, and good governance.

At the same time, we must recognize that a peripheral strategy alone will not suffice. The problems at the core of the Islamic world are simply too pressing, and the invasions of Afghanistan and Iraq—not to mention Iran's acceleration of its nuclear program and Saudi Arabia's continuing export of Wahhabism to the Islamic periphery—have created a new dynamic in the region. The danger is that, despite what is actually a remarkably successful series of counterinsurgency campaigns since the September 11 attacks, the United States will suffer from fatigue and withdraw from the region in the hope of a new stability. Such stability, however, would be illusory and, at best, temporary; the enemy, which has been under constant pressure, will use any respite to rearm, reorganize, and plot new attacks. The status quo regimes will believe, as they want to believe (and history has given them good reason to believe), that the United States has again lost interest in the region. Our allies, including those in the region who yearn for a better, freer life, will draw similar conclusions.

The United States cannot afford an "exit strategy," either from Iraq and Afghanistan or from the region as a whole. Neither can it afford a status quo strategy; the entrenched political order is itself the problem. Thus, the trend since 1979 of larger, longer, and more decisive U.S. military operations in the region must continue. The costs and dangers of military engagement at the core of the Islamic world will be high, exceeded only by the costs of withdrawal.

In sum, the conflict within the greater Middle East is a multifront war. American strategy for the region must proceed from the determination to build the capacity to operate in remote and widely separate locations. Although these operations may rarely take the form of direct invasion and regime change as in Iraq, the United States must retain the capability to undertake such operations if necessary, quite apart from its baseline engagement missions across the region.

Military Strategy to Shape China's Rise to Power. The growing wealth and power of the People's Republic of China have been increasingly apparent elements in international politics throughout the post–Cold War period. China's rise could not have been possible but for the collapse of the Soviet Empire; Beijing's break with Moscow provided the strategic framework for its embrace of economic modernization, and the great-power peace of the past fifteen years has helped sustain and accelerate that trend while allowing China to wield more political clout. At the same time, the PRC stands as a potential strategic competitor to the United States.

It is neither inevitable that China will be hostile to the United States or the American-led international order nor certain that China will achieve genuine great-power status. At the same time, U.S. strategy makers must concede that that balancing act between accommodating China's economic growth—indeed, encouraging it—and resolving Chinese political and strategic aspirations will be a precarious one. The United States wants to see a prosperous China and a free China. The Chinese people deserve no less, and American principles and interests insist on it.

Thus, it is essential that American military strategy strive to contain Chinese militarism, that is, to discourage any attempt by Beijing to gain by force or threat of force what it cannot otherwise obtain. This strategy most certainly includes territorial conquests, beginning with Taiwan. But U.S. strategy must also, in the longer run, concern itself with China's capability to confound American interests elsewhere. We must begin to regard Beijing not simply as a regional actor but increasingly as a factor in global geopolitics. China's growing power is, in tremendous measure, a function of a globalized economic system secured by American global military power. The distinction between global power and regional strength is vanishing.

China's great-power pretensions have been recognized by the Department of Defense since the late 1990s. The first sentences of the Pentagon's 1999 *Annual Report on the Military Power of the People's Republic of China* declared that "China's primary goal is to become a strong, modernized, unified and wealthy nation. It views its nation's standing in relation to the position of other 'great powers.' Beijing clearly wants to be recognized as a full-fledged great power."[13] The Clinton administration, despite its efforts to treat China as a "strategic partner," was forced to conclude that Beijing's strategic views were based on a "calculus" that U.S. policy intended to "restrict" Chinese power and "complicate China's effort to become the preeminent power in Asia."[14] Chinese military strategy was likewise primarily intended to "prepar[e] for capabilities the United States might bring to bear in any conflict."[15] In other words, China regarded the United States as its long-term enemy.

These facts did much to shape the initial military strategy and defense planning of the Bush administration; preparing for conflict with China underlay a good deal of the rationale behind the 2001 Quadrennial Defense Review and the program of transformation. And indeed, the 2004 edition of the Chinese military power report represents a development of these basic themes— China continues to see itself "emerg[ing] as a great power and the preeminent power in Asia"—and at the same time a more sophisticated understanding of Chinese strategy.[16] The new report recognizes that "China has had a longstanding geopolitical challenge in maintaining control over the heartland of China and major elements of 'inner Asia.'"[17] Yet China "has also sought to secure the vast periphery of coastal and land boundaries, as well as maritime territory in a region populated by traditional rivals and enemies."[18] Beijing's goal is to preserve a favorable "strategic configuration of power"—in other words, a balance of power, at least in East Asia, rather than the dominance of a single power, the United States.[19] Thus, Chinese leaders have long spoken about the desirability of a multipolar world order.

Many in East Asia, and even globally, have begun to accord great-power status to China. According to the Pentagon, "Beijing views itself as operating from an increasingly competitive position relative to other established world powers, including the United States."[20] This is a reflection of both China's own rise and the new realities of the post–September 11 world. Beijing clearly regards the global war on terrorism as creating a "strategic window of opportunity," wherein the new American "focus on counterterrorism has reduced perceived U.S. 'pressure' on and 'containment' of China, opening opportunities to strengthen internal security and create a more favorable situation along the periphery."[21] At the same time, American actions, particularly those resulting from the invasion of Afghanistan, have created new potential problems:

> China's leaders appear to have concluded that the net effect of the U.S.-led campaign has been further encirclement of China, specifically by placing U.S. military forces in central Asia, strengthening U.S. defense relations with Pakistan, India and Japan, and returning the U.S. military to Southeast Asia. . . . Because of these perceptions of Washington's strategy and presence Beijing believes U.S. intervention in conflict scenarios involving China . . . is increasingly likely.[22]

The most notable feature of this new turn in Chinese strategy is Beijing's increasing interest and presence in the greater Middle East. Energy security is becoming a central concern as China's economy continues to grow and industrialize. China is now the world's second-largest energy consumer and third-largest net oil importer, more and more dependent on outside sources of supply. As the United States–China Economic and Security Review Commission reported to Congress in June 2004, "China has a growing sense of insecurity because of increased dependence on tanker-delivered Middle East oil via sea lanes, including the Straits of Malacca and Hormuz, controlled by the U.S. Navy."[23]

Energy shortages are a paramount concern for Beijing, which is already having to ration its electric power supply, slowing the manufacturing economy and threatening overall economic growth. Thus, China's strategic horizons are expanding to prioritize "maintaining access to natural resources and markets and pursuing a 'counter-containment' strategy by establishing a regional presence and influence to balance and compete with the United States."[24]

Moreover, the problem will be exacerbated with time; China's share of world oil consumption is projected to grow significantly, with consumption doubling and perhaps tripling by 2010.[25] Thus, China is planning to create a strategic petroleum reserve, is pursuing a variety of pipeline deals with Central Asian states, and, most ominously, is seeking "non-market reciprocity deals with Iran, Sudan and other states of concern, including arms sales and WMD-related technology transfers that pose security challenges to the United States."[26]

In keeping with its political and strategic view, Beijing has an autarkic energy policy, which is "focused on owning the import oil at the production source."[27] This has the effect of creating strategic partnerships between China and those states that supply it with oil. The United States, by contrast, takes a market-driven approach to energy, and through its security policies, particularly toward the oil states of the Persian Gulf and the greater Middle East, has attempted to maintain influence from a distance. Thus, as Energy Department official James Caverly bluntly puts it: "Geopolitically, this could soon bring the United States and Chinese energy interests into conflict. Both countries will be in the Persian Gulf for oil."[28]

In sum, the United States needs to fashion a strategy for China that is itself nearly global in scope. Although centered on East Asia and the flashpoint along the Taiwan Strait, this strategy must also take account of China's interests and rising posture in the greater Middle East. Moreover, the United States should consider the prospects of an asymmetric response to provocative Chinese actions in East Asia, as the defense of U.S. interests in East Asia might in fact begin in the Persian Gulf, Central Asia, Southeast Asia, or even Latin America.

2

Missions

The emerging U.S. military strategy suggests five core missions for U.S. armed forces: defending the American homeland; fighting the global war on terror and transforming the greater Middle East; limiting the geopolitical effects of growing Chinese military power; responding to unforeseen contingencies; and continuing the transformation of the armed services.

Homeland Defense

Defense of the homeland has always been the prime directive for American strategy makers. Yet more than three years after the attacks of September 11, 2001, a useful meaning of "homeland defense" for the twenty-first century is still proving elusive for Pentagon planners. There is no question but that traditional distinctions between missions of homeland defense, which are external and fall to the military, and internal missions of homeland security, which fall to other institutions and instruments of the American government, are naturally blurred by the nature of the global war on terror. At the same time, however, some sense of clarity must be reclaimed. In particular, white-paper proposals to reconfigure the Army National Guard—already torn between its state and federal roles—into an instrument for consequence or crisis management in the event of another catastrophic terrorist attack inside the United States are unwise. Not only is it dangerous to bog down too much military power with assignments at home, but also it further erodes traditional civil-military relations, which have been on increasingly infirm ground through the post–Cold War years.

But even though the military role in direct homeland defense should be a narrow one, the traditional interpretation of the "American homeland" should not be wholly abandoned. The 9/11 attacks had the predictable and proper consequence of focusing policymakers' attention on the Middle East, even at the expense of other regions, including the Western Hemisphere, particularly from the Caribbean basin and Central and South America. These points are historically regarded (as in the Monroe Doctrine and the Roosevelt Corollary) as important to the defense of the continental United States, and they remain strategically valuable today. Even as the Pentagon concentrates its energies increasingly toward the greater Middle East, it cannot afford to wholly neglect our own backyard.

Indeed, the great strategists of the nineteenth century recognized that American hegemony in the hemisphere was critical to U.S. national security. Then, the foremost concern of national security theorists such as John Quincy Adams (the actual author of the Monroe Doctrine) was to prevent a European great power from taking advantage of a political and military vacuum elsewhere in the Americas to establish a foothold within striking distance of the United States. The Soviet Union recognized America's vulnerability in its strategic rear and repeatedly tried to establish beachheads in Latin America—from the deployment of nuclear missiles in Cuba in the 1960s to the support of the Sandinistas in Nicaragua during the 1980s.

Today, as well, the United States should not be sanguine about the weakness and instability of political actors along its southern rim and the possibility they could once again be exploited by America's enemies. In the context of the global war on terror, there is a long-standing concern that lawless regions of Latin America such as the Isla de Margarita in Venezuela and the Triborder Area (TBA), where the borders of Argentina, Paraguay, and Brazil meet, are being used by Middle Eastern radicals as safe havens.[1] The TBA, for instance, has long been recognized as a regional hub for Hamas and Hezbollah fund-raising, in addition to drug and weapons trafficking, smuggling, and document and currency fraud. Indeed, economic forces have created a huge market across Latin America and the Caribbean for fake passports, visas, and other identity papers that could be exploited by terrorists seeking to enter the United States undetected.

Latin America also presents an opening for strategic competitors today, much as it did earlier for the Soviet Union. China's interest in Latin America and the Caribbean is growing rapidly. Beijing is interested foremost in the region's natural resources—in particular, oil contracts in Venezuela, Colombia, and Ecuador—using "yuan diplomacy" and low-visibility military-to-military relations to style itself as an attractive political and economic counterweight to the United States. In the course of a recent two-week trip through the region, Chinese President Hu Jintao announced more than $30 billion in new investments and long-term contracts.[2] Although still a lower priority for China than Africa, the Western Hemisphere is unquestionably an area of rising strategic interest for the People's Republic, as reflected in China's recent decision to deploy troops to Haiti.

The Bush administration, to its credit, has expanded joint military exercises with Latin American forces, doubling the number of U.S. personnel helping the Colombian government wage its war with narco-guerrillas. It has also entered into a number of multilateral frameworks for dealing with hemispheric security issues, including a recent partnership with Chile and Panama to protect the Panama Canal—still a critical piece of infrastructure for commerce in the Western Hemisphere—from terror threats, while an even larger multinational force has been assembled for combined maritime patrol of the Caribbean basin.

Another critical element of the Pentagon's contribution to homeland defense is its missile defense programs, for which the 2005 QDR must provide a clear rationale. For too long, missile defenses have been treated as an end in themselves. The Clinton administration, animated by an outdated "arms control" mentality formed during the Cold War, failed to advance the rather limited but intelligent set of programs it inherited from the first Bush administration; rather than run the political risk of terminating them, it sought simply to reduce funding while dragging its feet. The second Bush administration, by contrast, has had an equally single-minded approach: undo the damage and root programs so deeply in the budget that killing them would be impractical. It also had a leftover Cold War agenda of its own—withdrawing from the ABM Treaty and negotiating reduced nuclear arsenals with Russia.

Treating missile defense as the last battle of the Reagan years has left a whole host of programs with a very uncertain strategic purpose in the post-9/11 environment. In a time of terrorism, the threat of ballistic missiles seems less pressing. The arsenals of rogue regimes such as North Korea and Iran appear to be intended as a (mostly indirect) deterrent to U.S. attack. Thus, although theater missile defenses remain an important priority, the argument for national missile defense would seem to have little immediate application to such antagonistic but essentially weak adversaries.

The real value of national missile defenses lies in the strategic competition with China. The PRC is estimated to have an arsenal of, at most, just a few dozen nuclear-armed intercontinental ballistic missiles. But the geopolitical consequences of a "deterred United States" that result from the possession of a minimal nuclear capability are exponentially worse than its actual capacity for physical destruction. North Korea, evil and dangerous as it is, cannot be construed as a great-power challenger to the United States and the global, liberal international order. The real mission for U.S. missile defenses is to eliminate the deterrent value of China's long-range ballistic missiles.

This is a mission, however, that there is deep institutional reluctance to acknowledge. Although China certainly commands the engineering talent and the wealth necessary to offset the U.S. investment in defenses, simply raising the cost of an assured deterrent for Beijing would add a crucial element to the larger strategic competition. To begin with, it would stand as a clear signal of American resolve to integrate China within the current world system rather than distort the system to suit the Chinese. The fundamental strategic premises of any long-term but indirect competition with China would be essentially and very favorably altered from the anti-Soviet Cold War. Second, the defensive nature of such systems is hardly provocative; China could never credibly claim that U.S. missile defenses were targeted at them, even though Beijing will certainly raise a diplomatic storm in order to preserve its cheap deterrent. Third, China would have to respond by investing in its offensive capabilities, creating significant opportunity costs for its program to develop conventional power-projection capabilities. Missile defense optimized to deal with a Chinese threat is a perfect example of an asymmetric approach to a very severe strategic challenge.

The Greater Middle East

Although defense of the homeland is the primary mission of U.S. armed forces, the missions that will most determine the overall shape of the military—and consume the largest portion of defense spending—are those that focus on the greater Middle East: the war against radical Islamist networks and the extended commitment to reshape the region's political order in a liberal and democratic fashion.

These two missions cannot be disentangled from each other. Indeed, perhaps the most useful departure for grasping this reality would be a thorough review of Operation Enduring Freedom in Afghanistan. Although not yet a complete victory, this mission has been a remarkable success—providing instructive lessons for planners and strategists of U.S. military force who are contemplating exactly what a "generational commitment" and a "long, hard slog" in the greater Middle East are likely to mean.

Above all else, Operation Enduring Freedom indicates that regime change resulting in democracy is no fantasy. Afghanistan under the Taliban established itself as one of the most repressive places in the greater Middle East. It was the revolutionary forefront of Islamic radicalism, the scene of a totalitarian political order. Yet just three years after the U.S. invasion, the Afghan people's enthusiastic embrace of elections and palpable political and economic progress stand as a stark rebuke to those who argue that military intervention and democratic transformation are mutually incompatible. Indeed, Afghanistan's elections would be unthinkable but for the removal of the Taliban by force of American arms, and the success of Afghan democracy is directly proportionate to the security made possible by U.S. peacekeepers and U.S.-trained Afghan soldiers. Although it is safe to say that the Bush administration did not, and cannot, "impose" democracy on Afghanistan, it did install a liberal-minded interim government—rather than a warlord—more likely to promote and respect it.

Second, the mission did not end once the Taliban were scattered. It is not just that Taliban and al Qaeda remnants continue to operate in remote regions or out of Pakistan's northwest provinces. It is that the mission of regime change itself demanded nothing short of a massive transformational effort. Had the United States withdrawn prematurely from Afghanistan, it is likely that the Taliban would have reconstituted itself and made another violent bid for power or that the country would have descended into internecine fighting among various factions. Operation Enduring Freedom thus required a larger and longer-term commitment of U.S. forces than originally anticipated, to both stabilize and democratize Afghanistan. Of note, the U.S. contingent in Afghanistan for the "postwar" period is substantially larger than that required for the invasion, having steadily crept upward to a strength of more than 12,000—with surges to roughly 20,000 in time of potential crisis, such as the recent presidential election.

American security strategy thus requires more than containment or even a "rollback" of enemies in the greater Middle East; it demands that we establish something more lasting in partnership with local allies. The job for our forces is to create the opportunity for these more representative, liberal, and ultimately stable governments to take root. In sum, although it is fairly easy to topple the decrepit governments of the region, and we are learning how to obstruct terrorist operations aimed directly at the United States, the mission in the greater Middle East is a larger one.

As our experience in Iraq suggests, neither the Bush administration nor the broader American political class has fully digested this apparently obvious lesson. In its outlines, Operation Iraqi Freedom has closely paralleled the campaign in Afghanistan: stunning initial success followed by an open-ended security commitment. But by contrast with its experience in Central Asia, the Bush administration was slow to engage in Iraqi postwar politics and reluctant to admit that any truly representative government would be led by the Shia majority. The administration was also slow to recognize or embrace traditional Shia leaders such as Ayatollah Ali al Sistani, the man who has proved to be our most constant ally in Iraq. And finally, we were hesitant to return nominal sovereignty to Iraqis; indigenous Iraqi leaders may be imperfect, to be sure, but a vast improvement on direct American rule.

This does not mean that U.S. strategy for the greater Middle East is simply to prioritize the list of countries to be invaded, occupied, and transformed. It does mean, however, that the exercise of military power—whether through direct or indirect means—is the sine qua non for long-term success. It will be far better to pressure despotic regimes to reform, and in strategically key states such as Pakistan or Saudi Arabia, there is hardly any other choice. Yet there can be no serious strategy for remaking the greater Middle East that does not hold out the prospect of regime change, essentially unilaterally, at the discretion of the United States. More important from a force-planning perspective should be the realization that the United States requires the unambiguous capacity to conduct such operations—particularly post-invasion operations—at the times and places of its own choosing and will continue to require such capacity in the future. And this, in turn, must define what the transformation of America's military capabilities actually means.

China

The third set of missions facing the U.S. armed forces relates to the growing geostrategic ambitions and military power of the People's Republic of China. In the 2001 Quadrennial Defense Review, China was regarded as an emerging regional power, in particular posing a mounting threat to Taiwan. In the intervening years, this danger has only grown; duty in the Middle East has repeatedly diverted U.S. forces from the western Pacific, and the Bush administration's attempts to modernize the Taiwanese military have faltered for a variety of reasons. Most significant, the pursuit of the war on terror has introduced uncertainty about China policy, as the Bush administration is understandably eager not to antagonize Beijing when its attention is already fully consumed by the wars in Iraq, Afghanistan, and the broader Middle East. The seeming clarity of the last QDR thus dissolved into confusion.

It is also the case that China's aggregate military power is far less than that of the United States. Nonetheless, Beijing now has capabilities—particularly quick-strike forces opposite Taiwan—that make the immediate, local balance of military power far less certain. The combination of short-range ballistic and cruise missiles, select naval forces, strike aircraft, and special-operations forces make a decapitating strike against Taipei an increasingly viable option. And even should Taiwan successfully upgrade its defenses—a very uncertain process and one that will take the better part of a decade, at best—the key question under such a scenario is the response of U.S. forces, especially naval and air forces.

The mission for U.S. forces is to have the credible capacity to respond to Chinese action against Taiwan within a very short time, preferably to stem a crisis short of war but certainly to act if hostilities begin. The rapidity of the response can only be fully judged in political terms: What would China perceive as a credible response? How would Taiwanese political leaders react? Measuring what constitutes an adequate response is naturally imprecise. However, if an initial Chinese strike goes unanswered for three or four days, it may be difficult to save the situation.

Steaming naval forces from distant stations may not be quick enough.

The U.S. response must be not only rapid but also sustained. Having once begun an attack, Beijing will not have very many attractive options for retreat, and the domestic consequences for the communist regime might well be very great. Chinese leaders must be convinced that further military operations would be entirely futile, resulting in catastrophic failure. An initial defeat at the hands of intervening American forces may cause a pause in the Chinese campaign, but it cannot guarantee a complete cessation of hostilities, even if the negotiated outcome is to be a return to the status quo ante. Thus, relying entirely on air forces is an uncertain option. Moreover, employing land-based aircraft stationed in Japan or even Korea will threaten to involve those nations in the conflict, immediately adding political complications. Nor is there any guarantee that Taiwanese airfields—certainly among the first targets of a Chinese strike—will be available.

By the same token, long-range aircraft based in the United States will be able to contribute only marginally. B-2 bombers or other strike aircraft have no direct air-defense role; their value would be in striking Chinese targets. Because these targets would be located on the Chinese mainland, such strikes might well be viewed as an escalation of the conflict; certainly Chinese leaders would regard them as such. There would be operational questions as well. For example, should counteroffensive strikes concentrate on hard-to-find mobile missile launchers, forward airfields, or command and control nodes?

In sum, any successful defense of Taiwan—and thus a credible deterrent to Chinese attacks or coercive diplomacy—requires a significant commitment of U.S. forces, including naval forces constantly within range or directly "on station." The Taiwan Strait occupies something equivalent to the Fulda Gap during the Cold War; it is a key geographical feature with great operational significance but even greater strategic and political significance. This spot requires a robust "forward defense"—meaning that, ideally, U.S. land-based air forces, missile defense units, and command facilities should be placed on the island. Unfortunately, our outdated China policy prevents that, and thus, for a host of reasons, this mission is a key element in sizing, shaping, and posturing the U.S. Navy for the future.

But as observed above, the full mission of hedging against expanding Chinese strategic ambitions and military influence does not end in the western Pacific. Perhaps Beijing's greatest strategic weakness is the disparity between its "out-of-area" interests and its extremely limited power-projection capacity. At the same time, Beijing has long exploited arms sales, proliferation networks, and other indirect means to extend its geopolitical reach and has proved itself more than willing to partner with rogue governments or to play both sides of the India-Pakistan divide.

Moreover, China is becoming a more persistent presence in the region surrounding the Indian Ocean. China has gradually been building up its military capabilities in Burma—yet another truly noxious regime—and clearly wants to develop a capacity to intervene along the energy supply route from the Persian Gulf through the Indian Ocean and through Southeast Asia. This is not simply a long and very vulnerable line of communication for China, but a reflection of Beijing's view that energy security is a central strategic concern. The United States, and in particular the U.S. Navy, must take these developments into account when calculating its own presence requirements.

Contingencies

None of the previous three quadrennial defense reviews has found a way to plan for contingencies. The 1997 review commissioned a very useful study, titled "Dynamic Look," which reviewed the then-short history of U.S. military involvement in the post–Cold War world as a way to try to quantify the unknown and uncertain. Despite the inherent difficulties of such an effort, its basic premise—that America's position as sole superpower and guarantor of the global order meant constant involvement in unforeseen contingencies—was sound. Alas, the 2001 review dispensed with the effort entirely, seeking refuge in trying to build military capabilities in the abstract rather than trying to forecast contingent missions.

The experience of the Bush administration strongly suggests the validity of the "Dynamic Look" model. It is not simply that the administration's initial desires to withdraw from the contingency commitments of the 1990s—most notably in the Balkans—have gone unfulfilled. Indeed, more than a decade after the retreat from Somalia, U.S. forces find themselves back in the Horn of Africa on a more or less permanent footing. And, of course, Marines are once again peacekeeping in Haiti.

The 2005 Quadrennial Defense Review must recapture this sense of retaining—or re-creating—forces capable of responding to unforeseen but urgent circumstances. The characteristics of such contingencies should be fairly clear. They require less by way of firepower and more by way of airlift, sealift, and mobile ground forces. Furthermore, nation building often has a second phase, even when there is no counterinsurgency combat as in Iraq. Even if U.S. combat forces play a supporting role in an international coalition, there is often a logistics demand that, at least for some time, can be met only by U.S. forces.

The attacks of September 11, 2001, have in large degree clarified the geopolitical challenges of the future, but the immensity of the challenge in the greater Middle East—and the mercurial character of modern terrorism—places a great value on having an unquestioned contingency capability. The deepening involvement of special operations forces, Marines, and airborne units (the traditional contingency response forces) in Iraq and Afghanistan call the U.S. quick-response capability into question.

Transformation

Four years ago, transformation of the U.S. military was regarded as the Department of Defense's prime mission. Candidate George W. Bush promised to "skip a generation" of weapons and hired

Defense Secretary Donald Rumsfeld to lead the charge on what was perceived as the status quo.[3]

In summary terms, the transformation project thus far has pursued operational goals. As suggested above, it has stressed a shift to an asymmetric, capabilities-based approach, following Rumsfeld's dictum that, although we may not know who our next enemy will be, we know how we would like to fight him. There have been a few strategically relevant new initiatives, such as the conversion of Trident ballistic-missile submarines to the "SSGN" configuration, loading these boats with Tomahawk cruise missiles, and some "persistent" reconnaissance and surveillance platforms such as the space-based radar and E-10 aircraft. Some new programs have also been initiated, such as the navy's Littoral Combat Ship, that may be valuable for other reasons but of questionable value to stated transformational goals. Most notable—if more for their controversy than for their actual transformational value—have been divestments such as the cancellation of the army's Crusader howitzer and Comanche helicopter. Finally, there has been a little repackaging of such on-the-books programs as the navy's DDX next-generation destroyer, which is now the SC-21 next-generation "surface combatant." In brief, there's been far more continuity than change.

Perhaps what is most curious is that the Rumsfeld transformation project is the part of the U.S. defense establishment that seems least responsive to the new, post-9/11 world. It is still fixated on long-range firepower when the demand is for ever more manpower operating at dangerously close range. It seeks a "transparent" battlefield where perfect information substitutes for armored protection; the so-called Office of Force Transformation has even published a critique of the famous armored "thunder runs" that transformed the battle of Baghdad from a lengthy siege into a blitzkrieg that finally drove Saddam Hussein from power. Yes, the tanks were brutally effective, concluded the report, but it would have been preferable to employ lighter forces, given timely intelligence from a fleet of unmanned aerial vehicles.

The 2005 QDR should proceed from the viewpoint that not all transformation is useful and that the measure of utility is derived from the geopolitical missions outlined above. That said, it makes sense to continue to regard transformation and experimentation as a separate mission, in the sense of requiring dedicated forces not immediately engaged in combat duties. Indeed, the army is having difficulty accomplishing its reorganization away from ponderous divisions into more effective, brigade-size "units of action" because Iraq is consuming so much of the available force. The upcoming review must also shed the notion that transformation means saving money and eliminating manpower. High technology is a wonderful thing and a strategic imperative for a military force with global responsibilities, but it is not a panacea that can save us from the nature of war.

3

Posture

The history of the United States is a case study in expansionism. From its origins as a diverse and often squabbling handful of English colonies in the western wilds of the British Empire to its current position of global hegemony, America has had a habit of looking outward to solve its security problems. The past century saw the expansion of our perimeter into air and space; the new century is pushing our interests into cyberspace. There is no immediate reason to expect American expansionism to end.

Accompanying this expansion of the American security perimeter has been a growing network of military facilities, both along the frontier and internally. Installations such as forts Riley and Leavenworth in Kansas were once outposts for Indian fighting, part of Andrew Jackson's "permanent Indian frontier" plan, then "hubs" for further force projection. In the 1880s, Fort Leavenworth became the home of the Army Staff College; Fort Riley has for some decades been the home of the First Infantry Division, a unit with much service in Germany and in the Persian Gulf. In Germany, Ramstein Air Base, near the front line during the Cold War, is now a key pillar in the American air "bridge" that makes the U.S. Air Force's boast of "global reach" a reality. The general pattern has been that, when one war ends, the United States fortifies the furthest reaches of the final front lines, and, when the next war begins, it builds new facilities to support still farther-flung operations.

Thus, it should hardly be a surprise, on the conclusion of the Cold War and the rise of a new series of threats to U.S. security interests, that the network of American installations should evolve. Had the wars in Afghanistan and Iraq not intervened, the Bush administration already would have begun to implement its plan for a new "permanent American frontier" and prepare for the congressional knife fight posed by the domestic Base Realignment and Closure (BRAC) process, set to begin this year. Yet even as the reality of the September 11 attacks and the global war on terror has turned the transformation of the Pentagon's global force posture into a strategic imperative of American national security, significant challenges—diplomatic, fiscal, and political— still stand in the way.

Bridges Not Far Enough

The Bush administration deserves credit for beginning to tackle the overdue work of reposturing our forces overseas; the Clinton administration had little interest in the issue, happy to avoid the diplomatic costs inherent in withdrawing and repositioning U.S. troops stationed in Western Europe or Korea. At the same time, however, the Bush Pentagon's plan, like the rest of its defense program, has become a partial captive to the hope that the missions in Afghanistan and Iraq are temporary anomalies. Although bold and ambitious in many ways, it is still only a first step.

Although the administration has yet fully to reveal its plans or much of a timetable, it has thus far made clear that it intends to reduce the garrisons in Germany and Korea significantly, withdrawing at least 25,000 to 30,000 troops from Europe and almost 15,000 from the Korean peninsula. That will leave about 35,000 U.S. soldiers in Germany and about 25,000 in South Korea. Moreover, many of the troops in Korea will be repositioned away from the demilitarized zone to the south, below Seoul. Such a move will not only render U.S. forces less vulnerable to a first strike by Pyongyang but also facilitate their redeployment in the event of contingency operations elsewhere in Asia. The European contingent will likewise be reconfigured, with new "lily-pad" transitory bases built in southeastern Europe, making it easier to support "out-of-area" operations in the Caucasus, the Middle East, and Central Asia.

The Greater Middle East

The single greatest weakness of the Bush administration's rebasing plan is its failure to persuade both enemies and allies that the American presence in the Middle East is sufficient for the "long, hard slog" described by Defense Secretary Rumsfeld. U.S. forces in Iraq, for instance, currently operate out of more than a dozen major sites. Although continuing success in the counterinsurgency campaign may allow for a reduction of the 150,000-plus troops now in Iraq, no military commander counts on a full withdrawal. And even once the counterinsurgency inside Iraq is won, there will still be the matter of regional security. The American commitment to Iraq is growing, not waning, as the country moves toward democracy.

President Bush has often described Iraq as the "central front" in the war on Middle Eastern terror. Just as it was necessary to defend the front lines in Germany during the Cold War—and the rationale for "forward defense" was political and strategic rather than military and operational—so it will be necessary to defend the front in the Middle East. While the interim Iraqi government of Ayad Allawi was in no position to negotiate a long-term status-of-forces agreement—the legal framework that would establish the terms of a continued American military presence in the country—a legitimately elected Iraqi government may be able and ready to do so.

This does not mean that future U.S. bases need to be an in-the-face irritant to Iraqi nationalism. The backhanded benefit of Saddam Hussein's massive army was that it had plenty of airfields and other facilities stuck out in the desert. These will prove an ideal infrastructure for a continuing training and strategic partnership between the new Iraqi security forces and the United States, and they will generally facilitate long-term U.S.

operations. Although neither the current American administration nor any future one will be eager for more wars in the region, it is folly not to prepare for the possibility. The operational advantages of U.S. bases in Iraq should be obvious for other power-projection missions in the region. Sites in northern and western Iraq would be key to patrolling the porous Iraqi borders with Syria and Iran. Lesser facilities in the far south would simply be an expansion of other U.S. posts in the Persian Gulf and Kuwait.

A similar logic applies in Afghanistan. The recent election has legitimated the government of Hamid Karzai, and the Afghan president has proved himself remarkably adept at creating consensus while marginalizing rivals and warlords who pose a threat to democracy. Yet Kabul's hold on the provinces, never strong, is far from solid. Revived opium agriculture supplies local leaders with the income to buy weapons and maintain their militias, while Taliban and al Qaeda remnants still lurk, both in Afghanistan and in Pakistan's northwest frontier. Even though Afghanistan is further along the path toward stability and representative government than Iraq, it is still undeniable that a long-term American presence—happily and, we hope, in conjunction with NATO—remains a necessity.

Thus, it comes as no surprise that the Karzai government wants to establish a status-of-forces agreement. In combination with bases in the Persian Gulf and Iraq, a modest network of bases in Afghanistan would also allow the United States to help contain and deter Iran and China alike.

Indeed, the basing implications of the global war on terrorism go well beyond the Persian Gulf. They extend well into the former Soviet republics of Central Asia, where the United States established airfields after the September 11 attacks. The Bush administration has also come to accept that the peripheries of the war in Africa necessitate new basing arrangements. Thus, the Pentagon secured in late 2002 its first sub-Saharan garrison in Djibouti, located at the strategic chokepoint between the Red Sea and the Gulf of Aden, where more than 1,000 troops are currently deployed as part of the Combined Joint Task Force–Horn of Africa.

In sum, U.S. posture throughout the greater Middle East should be conceived of as a web of mutually supporting facilities that will serve three purposes: expressing the American long-term commitment to political change in the region, enabling the deployment of forces to points of crisis, and sustaining an expanding set of partnerships and alliances with friendly—and, better yet, free—governments.

The Far East and the Indian Ocean

The situation is much the same in regard to East Asia and maritime South Asia. Since the 2001 Quadrennial Defense Review, the Pentagon has acknowledged the need to hedge against the growing military power of the People's Republic of China. Unfortunately, U.S. force posture in this vast region remains hobbled by the closure of the major airfield and port facilities in the Philippines, part of the initial post–Cold War reductions in the early 1990s. Essentially, the American security perimeter remains open for several thousand miles, from the island of Diego Garcia in the western Indian Ocean to South Korea and Okinawa. Any confrontation with China would thus require U.S. forces first to deploy forward, ceding the initiative to Beijing.

In response to this problem, the Pentagon has been improving its facilities on Guam. Once considered the "trailer park of the Pacific," the 209-square-kilometer island today receives twice as much military funding as a decade ago, part of a plan to transform it into a power-projection hub for the region. These investments include dredging Guam's outer harbor, upgrading its wharves for munitions handling, and, as has been done recently, basing B-52s and three nuclear attack submarines there. Additional work is underway on a hangar for B-1 bombers, a war reserve material warehouse, and a new base security center.[1]

Although having facilities on Guam cuts five days off a Pacific crossing from Hawaii, its value is diluted by the fact that the island is still thousands of miles distant from the most likely crisis points in the region, especially the Taiwan Strait and the area east of the island. The current rebasing plan has considered establishing some position in northern Australia, but although such a location would ease operations in Southeast Asia, it, too, is far distant from China.

Instead, the Bush administration should begin applying the patience and persistent diplomacy necessary to gain access to additional basing sites closer to Taiwan—with the Philippines foremost in value. To be sure, an American military homecoming would require great delicacy on Washington's part and some time to accomplish, but given the operational and strategic value of the Philippines, it is time to begin laying the groundwork. And the 2002 campaign to suppress the Abu Sayyaf terrorists on Basilan Island should have reminded Washington and Manila alike of the need for strategic cooperation, even aside from the question of China.

If direct cooperation and American facilities on Taiwan remain too provocative, U.S. force posture in the region must be otherwise optimized to be able to operate around and over Taiwan in times of crisis, even as the Chinese try to deny access. In this regard, basing arrangements in Singapore, Vietnam, and Palau could prove to be of value. And although Taiwan is not the only potential point of conflict with China, it is nonetheless the natural fulcrum around which U.S. forces in the Pacific should be positioned.

The American Nucleus

Taken together, the emerging U.S. military stance abroad is, and should be, less a conglomeration of separate regional bases than the interlocking parts of a single unified global force posture. At the core of this structure are the military facilities in the United

States itself—a core that is in critical need of reform. And as controversial as it will be to reposture American forces abroad, it may be even harder to accomplish a similar task at home.

The most immediate hurdle is the forthcoming round of the BRAC process. It is also a great opportunity, however, in part because the administration's efforts to call attention to the issue of the military's overseas posture have changed the politics of domestic base closures and realignment. The Pentagon's plans to move forces out of Germany and South Korea and close installations in both places give a greater rationale for sacrifices at home. At the same time, the chance of furnishing a home to units withdrawn from overseas posts provides an argument for keeping domestic facilities open.

Moreover, it is an open question whether the BRAC process itself has lost legitimacy. The process worked well initially, principally because the authorizing legislation was built around an "all-or-none" mechanism. According to a plan drafted by former representative Dick Armey, the list of bases to be realigned or closed was to be considered as a total package, depriving Congress of the ability to consider individual cases separately. But after the losses in the 1994 elections, the Clinton administration manipulated the subsequent round of base closings to permit two air force logistics centers in Texas and California, near closely contested districts and in key states, to "partially" close—that is, to remain open. Thus poisoned, the process ground to a halt, with the creation of a "depot caucus" in the House of Representatives adamantly opposed to further closures. It remains to be seen whether the political climate has changed, but the recent maneuverings of California governor Arnold Schwarzenegger, a popular Republican with real claims to have aided President Bush's reelection campaign, suggest that local political imperatives are still strong.[2]

Politics aside, several important strategic and operational considerations demand a reposturing of U.S. forces at home as well as abroad. Although the need to maintain American garrisons in far-flung corners of the globe is perhaps more crucial than ever, the new locations—the Middle East; Africa; Central, South, and Southeast Asia; and even southeastern Europe—are not nearly as suited to the kind of support structures common in Western Europe during the Cold War. It may be that, in time, these new bases can accommodate troops' families, military hospitals, and even the golf courses so beloved by officers, but that time is a long time distant. The continental United States is not simply the locus from which American military power is projected abroad; it will increasingly be where almost all American military families live. The pattern of army and air force troop rotations is now more like traditional navy and Marine Corps duty.

Despite a decade's worth of incremental improvements, it is uncertain whether, as a whole, U.S. installations are capable of sustaining an expanded and extended rotational posture for units abroad. The arithmetic of power projection is much the same for facilities as it is for troops: to maintain a base abroad requires a domestic infrastructure about five times larger. And, in fact, the advance of technologies allows many military command and logistics functions to operate at a greater distance, a trend that tends to increase stateside responsibilities and participation in overseas operations. Even some combat functions, such as the operations of long-endurance unmanned aerial vehicles, are now controlled globally from facilities at home. Just as the tactical "tooth-to-tail" ratio is changing, with a growing support "tail" for every trigger-pulling "tooth" (a pattern that continues despite the nature of close combat in Iraq and Afghanistan), the support of an expanding base network overseas will place greater demands on domestic installations. The administration wisely plans to better position overseas garrisons to reinforce "laterally" to crisis spots—as units from Europe have operated away from their home stations for years, units in Korea are being repositioned and restructured to do the same—but the core of U.S. power projection remains in the United States.

As noted above, another consideration is where to recruit, train, and station a larger force, most importantly a larger ground force. Any decision to expand the army's size carries with it the need to expand facilities. Part of the rationale behind the reductions of the early 1990s was supposed to be to preserve an "expansible" force, capable of rapidly mobilizing and absorbing larger numbers of troops in the event they were needed, but beyond lip service, no real effort was made to maintain such a capability. The upcoming BRAC process will have to begin to remedy this past neglect.

The potential double blow of a withdrawal of overseas-stationed forces and an overall expansion in the forces based at home compounds the problems and the expense. Frances Lussier of the Congressional Budget Office has estimated that the withdrawal and restationing of 14,000 soldiers from Korea would entail about $1.2 billion in infrastructure costs at home.[3] That suggests that expanding the army by 30,000 per year would add another $2.5 billion or so per year in such costs—not counting the cost of the manpower itself or the costs of equipping, training, and operating the larger force.

In sum, the posture of U.S. forces at home and abroad is one grand question; just as a global superpower needs a global strategy, it needs a genuinely global military posture. Getting all the right pieces in all the right places will be a long-term effort, constantly constrained by both domestic and international politics. Nevertheless, the second Bush administration must strive to set forth a coherent blueprint that gives some structure to the inevitable horse trading to come.

4

The Armed Services

The defense reviews of the post–Cold War era have had almost no measurable impact on the structures or programs of the U.S. armed services, other than to scale down the forces that previously existed. Moreover, the military's obsession with technology has left the services increasingly ill suited for the missions they must actually execute. As the cost of effective firepower has diminished dramatically, the Pentagon has sought to buy more firepower rather than complement these amazingly effective capabilities with equally effective maneuver abilities. Even when the maneuver dimension of warfare has been considered, it has been almost solely through the perspective of speed, with no regard for the other virtues of mass or sustainability. In sum, the current preferred American way of war is to dash about the planet, zapping its enemies from afar, and then prepare for the next sally. It is, essentially, a raiding strategy on a global scale, the sort of approach more fitting for lesser powers than superpowers.

Having in his first term committed the United States to the first major war of the twenty-first century, President Bush in his second term has an obligation to be sure that he begins to build the military forces needed to prevail in this conflict and preserve the larger international order, the Pax Americana. To accomplish this goal, the upcoming 2005 Quadrennial Defense Review must be built on an analysis of missions, not capabilities. Indeed, the primary value of these reviews is in their "illustrative scenarios"—the imagining of the wars U.S. forces might be called on to fight. The central problem of past reviews was that they clung to two scenarios—the canonical duo of an Iraq war and a war on the

Korean peninsula—far too much. The 2001 QDR at last began to give some consideration to a Taiwan Strait crisis, and this situation needs even greater focus in the 2005 review. But two newer scenarios must also be weighed in the balance: the continued war in the greater Middle East and the "nuclear nightmare" scenario, where a weak and potentially hostile nuclear state—Pakistan, North Korea, or, soon enough, Iran—acts in such a way where a military operation becomes unavoidable. It is not for the QDR to inquire too deeply into the political conditions that might lead to such a decision, but rather to try to consider the capabilities required for what would be a highly challenging mission. It should also attempt to understand these scenarios as true campaigns, conducted for some political purpose, rather than simply as punitive strikes.

By Their Scenarios Shall Ye Know Them

In the world of illustrative scenarios, strategy and policy meet military reality. In the U.S. defense establishment, as in most modern militaries, these exercises are where commanders confront the wars they are likely to fight and try to imagine how they would like to fight them. Working through scenarios also provides the basis for force-planning decisions. These exercises can be the best way to change—to genuinely transform—a military bureaucracy.

China. As indicated above, the 2005 QDR should be built around three core scenarios that go a long way toward capturing the range of missions implicit in the Bush administration's national security strategy. And although the Taiwan Strait scenario has become more familiar to defense planners over the past five years, it is an inherently dynamic one. The modernization of the Chinese People's Liberation Army (PLA) and its buildup of forces directly opposite Taiwan are changing the correlation of forces in the region very rapidly. Although the growth of China's ballistic- and cruise-missile force—now estimated to be about 600 in the immediate theater of operations and increasing constantly—has received the greatest attention, the challenge is far more complex.

Perhaps the most significant change from the 2001 QDR is the emergence of China's attack submarine fleet, a fact underscored by the detection of a Han-class nuclear submarine off Okinawa by the Japanese navy in November 2004. Complementing this capability, the PLA navy is assembling a force of destroyers. The effect of both these developments is to complicate the ability of the U.S. Navy to operate safely in the waters around Taiwan, particularly the deep water east of the island. A key operational goal for China is to construct a cordon around Taiwan, constraining American response in a crisis.

China's advances in strike-aircraft technologies are also notable. Even as it continues to build missiles designed to target Taiwan, the PLA air force recognizes the need to sustain operations beyond the effects possible by missile attacks of any realistic size. As in American doctrine, these capabilities are understood to be complementary and reinforcing. In addition to hitting key command nodes and political targets, a Chinese missile strike would also be intended as an air-defense suppression effort, to allow the improving-but-still-limited Chinese air force to prosecute a more extended air campaign against Taiwan.

Finally, the Chinese military is taking many of the steps necessary to harden, disperse, and otherwise ensure that its command system could continue to function even in the event of a limited war involving U.S. forces. Key Chinese facilities are increasingly located far inland, well out of the reach of land- and sea-based U.S. tactical-range systems. In essence, the size and scope of the potential Taiwan theater of operations are growing exponentially. Moreover, the power-projection capabilities being cultivated by the PLA threaten not only the Taiwanese but also other American friends and allies in the region.

Thus, the deterrent—or combat—task for U.S. forces under such a scenario is increasingly challenging. No longer can the U.S. Seventh Fleet simply sail through the Taiwan Strait. Perhaps the key to the entire campaign would be U.S. response time;

noting that in the "missile blockade" crises of 1995 and 1996 two weeks elapsed before the first U.S. naval forces arrived on the scene, China has strived to create a set of capabilities that would maximize the effect of bolt-from-the-blue strikes. Response time is not simply a measure of speed of transit, but proximity of initial dispositions. In other words, a Taiwan Strait scenario increases the importance of having forward-deployed U.S. forces in the western Pacific. Improved Chinese capabilities have also increased the size of the "battlespace" in which any U.S. response force must operate.

A key factor in this scenario must be the ability to immediately target sites on the Chinese mainland, and perhaps deep inland. The decisive phase might well be the one after an initial Chinese missile barrage, and the decisive act, in both political and operational terms, may be the ability to prevent the PLA air force from conducting an extended air campaign.

In sum, the United States must be able to put a significant force in the theater almost from the moment of the initiation of hostilities or at the first serious note of warning. This reaction is essential not only to deter a Chinese strike or to defend Taiwan in the event of such an attack but also to rally regional allies to support U.S. operations. A failure to react in a timely and strong way would cede the initiative to Beijing and invite defeat.

The good news about the Taiwan Strait scenario is that it is a classic, if very challenging, theater war scenario. It is the sort of war well understood by the Pentagon. The operational goal is to repel an attack and restore the status quo. There is no open-ended commitment to "regime change" or to the active transformation of the political order in China or anywhere else. The scenario's challenges are primarily military.

Terrorism. In contrast, the set of scenarios associated with the global war on terrorism (or "GWOT" in Pentagonese) are relatively modest in a military sense but immensely ambitious politically. The purpose of this conflict, as President Bush has made unmistakably clear, is to introduce liberal, democratic governments throughout the region. As noted above, the GWOT battlespace is similarly expansive, extending from maritime West Africa to the most inland parts of Asia to maritime Southeast Asia. Fortunately, American forces already possess the capability to set the initial conditions for long-term success.

The purpose of the 2005 QDR should be, perhaps above all else, to wrestle with the requirement to sustain and complete the victories in Iraq and Afghanistan. Not only are these efforts important in themselves, but the Pentagon must accept that the post-invasion phases of GWOT—the set of missions ranging from very violent counterinsurgency operations to more benign forms of nation building—are the decisive parts of these campaigns. The Department of Defense must further recognize that these sorts of constabulary efforts are exceedingly likely in the future. In contrast to the Taiwan Strait scenario, the challenge is not how fast we can get there, but how long we can stay.

Thinking about the GWOT must also give greater emphasis to engagement missions, particularly with those states and militaries in the region's emerging democracies. Many of these governments are dangerously weak and prone to corruption or military coup. Nonetheless, the value of nurturing even an embryonic strategic partnership more than repays the effort; U.S. armed forces must simply be sized and shaped for this purpose.

Nightmares. Finally, in addition to these two fairly predictable and unarguable scenarios, the 2005 QDR must begin to wrestle seriously with a range of nightmare scenarios, most often involving the presence or use of nuclear weapons. These nightmare scenarios call for a combination of the qualities that define the challenges of a showdown over Taiwan and GWOT: U.S. forces must not only deploy rapidly but also sustain a large-scale campaign aimed at a greater and more ambitious purpose than simply restoring the status quo. A brief discussion of one such potential scenario is illustrative of how tough these problems are.

In the Islamic Republic of Iran, the development or acquisition of nuclear weapons will make a dangerous regime even more dangerous. Strategically, such an arsenal threatens to nullify the strength of U.S. conventional forces. Of course, the country was not an inviting military target to begin with: size, rugged terrain, and a large population make Iran far less susceptible to invasion than Iraq.[1] Moreover, U.S. forces have plenty to do to complete the campaigns in Iraq and Afghanistan.

At the other end of the spectrum, punitive strikes or an Osirak-style raid (that is, operations similar to the 1981 Israeli airstrike against Iraq's Osirak nuclear facility) intended to set back the Iranian nuclear program could well have more costs than benefits. A strike would almost certainly rally Iranian opinion around a regime that otherwise has diminishing legitimacy and increasingly relies on periodic campaigns of repression against dissidents. Nor is it certain that a raid or series of raids would produce Osirak-like results. Iran's nuclear program is advanced far beyond the Iraqi program of the early 1980s, better dispersed, and specifically designed to withstand just such attacks. In any case, Iran would remain intact politically, perhaps more unified in the near term, and capable of retaliation against the United States, its allies, and its interests. The most inviting means of retaliation for Iran would be through terrorist proxies, and even if this response were not directed at the American homeland itself, it seems certain that Iran could reach throughout the greater Middle East and into Europe.

At the same time, this does not mean that the United States must remain inactive in the face of an Iranian nuclear threat. Our larger strategy in the region is premised on the active transformation of the political order, which, to succeed, must continue; fear of a nuclear Iran cannot be allowed to stall this process, and Tehran cannot be permitted to wield a veto over American policy in the greater Middle East. Moreover, it is folly to believe that Iran's purpose in acquiring nuclear weapons is solely to deter the United States. Rather, Iran's nuclear deterrent is intrinsically linked to its hegemonic aspirations in the Persian Gulf.

Thus, the QDR must define the qualities of a force capable of providing a solution instead of a stalemate and do so in a timely fashion. And although such scenarios ought to be strong factors in shaping the process of military transformation, it will take more than the invention of a new generation of wonder weapons to address a problem that is on the immediate horizon, not decades away.

Specifically, QDR planners must consider a range of limited-war options. These alternatives must go beyond punitive strikes, for they must be significant enough to seriously pressure the Iranian regime and present it with a continuing threat so as to discourage retaliation. A less-than-full-scale invasion, for instance—perhaps to establish enclaves in Iranian Kurdistan or in the Arab provinces in the south—while interrupting Iranian oil exports and production might suit these purposes. Such operations would not require the size of force or extended preparations (such as a large air-defense suppression campaign) as needed for a full invasion. The enclaves could provide rallying points for Iranian opposition, serving much as Northern Alliance territory did in Afghanistan and the northern no-fly zone did in Iraq.

Admittedly, a limited war would not eliminate the risks of war with Iran. Its sole virtue would be to raise the rewards to make them more commensurate with those risks and to do so within the scope of what might be militarily possible. Furthermore, such capabilities may be required in other scenarios, such as the breakdown of the government in Pakistan or in Saudi Arabia. Part of the purpose of defense reviews is to imagine nightmare scenarios and then think through how to deal with them. In an era of extremism, terror, and nuclear proliferation, it is myopic to do otherwise.

An Army for Regime Change

In a world illustrated by the scenarios described above, what is the role of the U.S. Army? Past defense reviews have often treated the army as an anachronism of the Cold War—too ponderous, too heavy, too blunt a tool for the high-tech wars of the twenty-first century. But despite the expanded roles played by special operations forces in the global war on terror, the ongoing campaigns in Iraq and Afghanistan feature conventional forces, both light and heavy. Neither campaign, in either country, has been rapid or yet politically decisive. Both Afghanistan and Iraq stand as evidence of the fundamental intellectual error of past defense reviews—especially the 2001 edition—and the enduring value of large and varied land forces capable of sustained operations lasting years.

A corollary to this past error has been that the focus of post–Cold War army modernization and transformation has been relentlessly tactical. Thus, the current reorganization of the force is centered on brigade-size "units of action"—the basic, self-sustaining atom of land power. Nothing is inherently wrong with this process, and the reforms now under way represent a reasonable response to technological change and the increasing availability of precision firepower. The effort, however, is essentially an ant's-eye view of the overall mission of the service. The 2005 QDR would do far better to take a broader review of the requirement for the sustained land power that is the core competency of the U.S. Army. The army's largest challenges are institutional and, in combat, at the highest level; the Pentagon needs to concentrate more on building a theater army for the long-running war in the greater Middle East rather than the perfect brigade. Indeed, the general thrust of Defense Department thinking about land forces has been misguided for more than a decade, a product of lessons mislearned from the experience of the Balkans in the 1990s. Thus, Major General James Dubik, considered "one of the intellectual fathers of Army transformation"[2] and a force behind the creation of "middleweight" units and the acquisition of the Stryker wheeled combat vehicle, could write as recently as October 2001:

> How many class-70 bridges [capable of supporting the weight on an M1 tank] exist, for example, between Germany and Bosnia? In Bosnia? How many between Albania and Kosovo? Perhaps more to the point: How

many are there in the potential deployment areas around the world? The answer: few, if any.[3]

This emphasis on deployability in particular and capability in general remains an intellectual fashion despite the centrality of heavy armored forces to the campaign in Iraq, both in the initial invasion and in subsequent counterinsurgency operations in urban areas. The mission of land combat vehicles involves more than shipping them or airlifting them to a remote theater and then driving across a bridge. As it has happened, seventy-ton tanks have been quite useful in Fallujah, as they were in the open field against the Republican Guard. Yet the Rumsfeld Pentagon has been reluctant to learn this lesson. Despite the assertion of a generational commitment to change in the Middle East, at least some observers believe it is "no longer possible to predict with high confidence where the Army will find itself deploying."[4]

The 2001 QDR thus demanded land forces that were lighter.[5] Even more than the effort to decrease the size and weight of modern tanks and fighting vehicles, however, there has been an ongoing effort to reduce the logistics tail associated with sustaining a large ground force. As Deputy Defense Secretary Paul Wolfowitz told Congress in 2002, large land forces

> depend on vulnerable foreign bases to operate—creating incentives for adversaries to develop "access denial" capabilities to keep us out of their neighborhoods. We must therefore reduce our dependence on predictable and vulnerable base structure, by . . . reducing the amount of logistical support needed by our ground forces.[6]

Yet, by invading Afghanistan and Iraq, the United States has, in the broadest strategic sense, already defeated the crucial attempt at "access denial" to the Persian Gulf region or the larger Middle East. In Iraq and Afghanistan, we have built—or rebuilt—a fair number of large bases; to be sure, they remain tactically vulnerable to mortars, suicide car bombers, and other attacks, but they are a measure of our strength rather than our weakness. Not only should we maintain them, we must. To use Wolfowitz's phrase, we are already in the enemy's "neighborhood," and we should plan to stay; indeed, staying should be the basis of our planning. And put plainly, this means rebuilding the active-duty army.

Numbers Matter. Before Iraq, military "transformationists" were fond of observing that manpower was a Napoleonic and outmoded measure of military effectiveness; victory no longer went to the big battalions. Not only was the overall active U.S. military reduced from 2.1 million in 1990 to 1.3 million by 2001, but most crucial, the active-duty army was cut from 780,000 to 480,000 soldiers in the same period.

Today, over 315,000 soldiers are deployed overseas.[7] More than 150,000 are in Iraq, and about 18,000 are in Afghanistan. The army relies very heavily on reserve and National Guard troops, who make up about 40 percent of the soldiers in Iraq. Although there is debate in the Pentagon, there is no reason to believe that a reduction to previous, prewar levels of deployment is soon to be achieved. Even if progress continues in Afghanistan and elections in Iraq bring a new legitimacy to the government in Baghdad, the United States must continue to support these fragile experiments in democracy in the Islamic world.

The current force is simply too small to sustain these commitments. By late 2004, almost four-fifths of the army's thirty-three brigades were deployed abroad, and soldiers in nine of the ten active-duty divisions were deployed to Iraq or Afghanistan, preparing to do so, or had just done so. Most notable, the units that had participated in the initial invasion of Iraq, such as the Third Infantry Division, 82nd and 101st Airborne divisions, and the Third Armored Cavalry Regiment, had either already been redeployed to the region or were about to redeploy. Tours of units in both Iraq and Afghanistan have routinely been extended, often for several months beyond the nominal one-year intended tour— a tour that is double the length that was considered preferable and sustainable in the Balkans during the 1990s and, of course, is now conducted in more violent conditions. Senator John Kerry did more than score debating points when, in the 2004 presidential campaign, he referred to the practice of stop-loss—retaining soldiers on active duty after their formal service commitment has expired—as a "backdoor draft."[8]

These extraordinary demands are felt most sharply among National Guard personnel and Army Reservists. Since September 11, 2001, of the 550,000 troops in the Army National Guard and Army Reserve, more than a quarter have typically been activated.[9] Approximately 200,000 are on active duty at the time this paper is written. Because army force structure relies heavily on the reserve components for combat support and combat service support tasks, and because these military job specialties have been in high demand throughout the post–Cold War period, many reservists have been deployed overseas as frequently as active-duty soldiers. The Maryland Army National Guard 115th Military Police Battalion, for example, has been on active duty for more than twenty-four months since 9/11 and deployed three times.[10]

To repeat: this level of land-force commitment ought to be considered the baseline for the future. Although troop levels in Iraq and Afghanistan may be safely reduced in time, it is almost impossible to imagine that the strategic goal in the region—the political transformation of the Islamic world—can be achieved soon or without the continued threat or use of force. Even when regime change can be accomplished peacefully or through swift invasions such as in Iraq and Afghanistan, the need to sustain and bolster allies and newly democratic governments will require significant manpower on the ground.

Judging the right size for the total army and particularly for the active-duty component—which is by far better suited to the conduct of long-term constabulary or stability operations—is more art than science. And ultimately these judgments will be shaped by cost constraints, both in budgetary and in social terms. Nevertheless, the experience of the past two years provides the salient data: To maintain this level of land-force effort, an active-duty army of 625,000 to 650,000 soldiers is required—an increase of 125,000 to 150,000 troops. Yet even a force of this size would not eliminate the requirement for complementary reserve components and continued calls of reservists to active duty.

This enlargement of the army is a necessary step—the single most important step—in closing the gap between our strategic ends and our military means.

Rebalancing the Active Force, Rebuilding the Service. Yet the army must not only be a larger force, but be a different force than it is now. Again, the focus of the QDR should be less on the tactical level, where the process of reform is advancing already, than at a higher echelon and, perhaps most important, at the level of the service institution itself.

As the experience of Iraq so dramatically demonstrates, the active-duty army relies heavily on the combat support and combat service support capabilities of the reserve components. But in truth, this has been an issue in every significant post–Cold War ground operation, beginning with the invasion of Panama in 1989.[11] Close observers of the army have long understood the imbalance between combat and support elements, particularly in constabulary and counterinsurgency operations.

At the same time, transformationists in the Pentagon have argued against the supposedly disproportionate logistical "tail" that encumbered modern land forces. Defense Secretary Rumsfeld, in particular, has been determined to break the army of its reliance on a heavy logistics structure, which in part explains the composition of the Iraq invasion force and its limited sustainability capability. The army has in turn made this wound even worse: the ratio of combat arms to support soldiers in its new Stryker brigades is 6 to 1 as opposed to about 2.5 to 1 in more-traditional units.[12]

Army experts have recognized that this is a potential difficulty for the hoped-for future force, which is to be lighter, more deployable, and designed for widely dispersed tactical operations. Indeed, the service's concept of operations for its Stryker brigades and its future force argue that these units "will need to . . . avoid vulnerable lines of communication while retaining operational momentum."[13] The danger foreseen—and so fully proved in Iraq— is that long lines of communication are vulnerable and require huge numbers of combat forces if they are to be fully secured; initial Iraq invasion planning, for example, identified several hundred positions to be defended by at least a platoon along the march route from Kuwait to Baghdad alone.

Thus, in expanding the active-duty army, most of the new manpower should be devoted to creating a sufficient support structure to sustain these sorts of widely dispersed operations, including, to some degree, the military police and infantry forces necessary to secure extended lines of communication. The army cannot simply imagine, as much of its emerging doctrine does, that aerial resupply can substitute for more traditional methods of logistics.[14] Neither the air force nor the army has, or is likely to acquire, such capabilities, particularly with the early termination of the C-130 program. Again, the army community understands the problem quite well, but in the rush to be seen as fully committed to transformation, some in the military have wished away the need for more robust logistics capability or have delegated the work to contractors. And although contractor support is proving essential in Iraq, and is on balance an option to be retained, it also creates significant strategic vulnerabilities. Contractors, for instance, have been a ready source of hostages and targets for insurgents in Iraq.

To stress here a point made more generally above: The army's immediate problems are less likely to be resolved by building better or more maneuverable brigades than by making its support commands more robust and building more truck companies. These formerly "rear area" troops find themselves as frequently on the front lines of operations in the Middle East. In the current and foreseeable future environment, the soldiers in these jobs must be as professional, as prepared for combat, and as well equipped as the airborne infantry, for they are as essential to the operational success of the force in the field and the overall strategic success of these kinds of missions.

Finally, if the field army must be larger and more robust, the same is also true of the institutional army, that part of the service that raises, trains, educates, and otherwise cares for the development and health of the field army. Over the past decade, the institutional army been stripped of manpower to sustain operations in the field, and its capacity has been severely compromised. During the force drawdown of the 1990s, efforts at recruitment received far less attention; the army "wasn't hiring." Now that the army needs soldiers, they are not so readily available. To meet its recruiting goals for 2004 for the active force, the army has had to lower its entry standards and dip into its pool of "delayed entry program" recruits. Recruiting for the reserve components did not meet its goal. The army's basic and other training facilities have likewise been reduced in scope, with important long-term consequences. According to Army Chief of Staff General Peter J. Schoomaker, the army cannot expand by much more than an additional 30,000 recruits per year, because of limitations in its logistical ability to train new soldiers. At that rate, it would take more than four years to train the additional 125,000–150,000 troops we need today. Army and military higher education has also been degraded by cost-saving distance learning methods and lessened investment in staff and war colleges. In general, the institutional army has been treated as a business would treat overhead expenses—as something to be pared to the bone and measured only as a drain on profits. Restoring the army to overall health requires that the institutional army receive as much attention as the field army.

A "Green Water" Navy

Of all the armed services, the U.S. Navy may ultimately be the most affected by the end of the Cold War and the unfolding American commitment to the greater Middle East. Since the rise of the United States as a world power late in the nineteenth century, the navy has been dedicated, first and foremost, to "blue water" missions—controlling the world's sea lines of communication to secure international commerce and to permit the projection of military power. This mission remains, but the very successes of the U.S. Navy over the past century have driven every military rival from the oceans; no other fleet, with the possible exception of the British navy, can be considered a global force. In retrospect, the Soviet Union's naval strategy was essentially a replay of the traditional strategy for a European continental power such as Germany: an attempt at a raiding strategy built on a strong submarine fleet.

Nonetheless, U.S. dominance of the world's sea lines of communication is not guaranteed in perpetuity, and it is possible to foresee the source of the most likely challenges. The two rising powers of the twenty-first century, China and India, both have maritime interests and ambitions. A centerpiece of U.S. strategy should be to develop a deeper strategic partnership with India, and given the fundamental consonance of geopolitical interests and democratic principles between Washington and New Delhi, such a partnership is a reasonable basis for defense planning. By contrast, although the United States shares many economic and geopolitical interests with China, the fact remains that Beijing is, at best, ambivalent about its role in an American-led international order. Therefore, maintaining maritime supremacy vis-à-vis China is the key "blue water" task for the U.S. Navy in the coming years.

The navy also has an important "brown water," or littoral, task associated with counterterrorism efforts and the effort to transform the greater Middle East. It is the maritime equivalent of ground force constabulary missions, patrolling the American security perimeter in such places as the Gulf of Guinea, the Gulf of Aden, the Red Sea, and Southeast Asia. It might even be said to be a kind of coast guard mission or even a transformed version of the navy's traditional "presence" activities. However it is to be characterized, it will certainly be a staple of U.S. Navy operations for the foreseeable future and thus a core mission demanding appropriate force planning.

The Navy in the Middle East. For more than fifteen years, the navy has carried a heavy burden of deployments in the Middle

East, most notably in the Persian Gulf. Indeed, the increased involvement of the U.S. military in the region can be said to have begun with Operation Earnest Will, involving the "re-flagging" of Kuwaiti tankers in 1987. Ever since that time, it has been U.S. policy to keep at least one aircraft carrier battle group more or less constantly on station in the region. Because of the delicacy of U.S. diplomacy and strategy in the Middle East, naval forces offered tremendous advantages—or, perhaps more accurately, avoided the difficulties associated with operations ashore that may have offended local sensibilities. And, especially in the first Gulf War and the subsequent, periodic moves against Saddam Hussein, naval strike power played an important operational role.

But beginning with Operation Iraqi Freedom and more obviously with the postinvasion counterinsurgency, the relative importance of naval forces has ebbed. To be sure, the war involved a huge naval force—seven carrier strike groups—and the air campaign included more than 800 Tomahawk cruise missiles, including 400 alone on March 21, 2003, and most of these missiles were fired from submarines.[15] More to the point, the value of the "shock and awe" strike efforts—the so-called strategic air campaign—seems in retrospect to be far from the decisive act it was intended to be. It did not unseat Saddam's regime, nor did it heavily affect the correlation of forces during the invasion itself; air support to the land maneuver forces was crucial, to be sure, but that job fell mostly to land-based aircraft. It is a telling statistic that the navy expended "less precision ordnance than expected" during the campaign; equally significant, the navy scaled back its purchases of laser- and satellite-guided bombs last year.[16]

Perhaps even more salient, the nature of the naval mission in the region is changing. Rather than providing firepower ashore or supporting land forces, the navy finds itself increasingly undertaking various forms of maritime patrol and intercept operations, helping to disrupt the movements and operations of terrorists and other radical factions, limit arms flows, defend against terrorism at sea, and conduct other similar missions. The area of such operations will be vast, from the West African coast to the South China Sea, and will require a sizable fleet as well as land-based maritime patrol aircraft. It will not, however, require that each vessel be as large or as sophisticated as modern or next-generation surface combatants, let alone nuclear submarines or aircraft carriers.

The Navy in Maritime South and East Asia. By contrast, the navy's role in containing the military power of the People's Republic of China demands the most sophisticated kind of fleet and still one sizable enough to maintain constant presence in the region. U.S. naval forces must provide the front line of deterrence—to be sure, supported by the air force—in situations where both the strategic and operational balance is weighted heavily in China's favor.

First of all, the navy must offset China's geographical advantages: China is there; the United States is far distant. Even forward-stationed naval forces, such as in Japan or on Guam, are far from potential flashpoints such as the Taiwan Strait. The advantages of geography also translate into operational advantages: the value of China's relatively short-range aircraft, missiles, and naval forces is maximized, as is the simple fact of their presence: they are *always* there, a potential threat. To respond, the United States must significantly expand the operational "tempo" and patterns of its naval forces. The size of the U.S. Pacific fleet should be expanded to include the majority of carrier groups, sophisticated surface combatants, and attack submarines. The western Pacific is the most likely locus of a "blue water" navy conflict.

Thus, the navy should reposture itself to ensure that several carrier task forces and other major combatant forces are in the region on a regular basis. At all times, at least one such formation should be within several days' sail—or less—of Taiwan; rapid response in times of crisis or actual combat is the key to a successful outcome should a conflict break out. As discussed elsewhere in this paper, this strategy will require an advanced and distributed basing posture throughout the region, much closer to crisis points than Hawaii or even Guam. At the same time, there should be depth and breadth to this basing posture in response to the growing inventory of longer-range Chinese missiles and the expanding capacity of the Chinese submarine fleet.

Finally, the navy must get serious about its role in ballistic-missile defense. The threat of these weapons is most volatile in East Asia, but not just because of the dangers posed by North Korea. Given its great-power aspirations, China has a tiny and antiquated force of long-range ballistic missiles; it enjoys deterrence— meaning deterrence of the United States—for a bargain-basement price. The Chinese understand this as a key to their expansionist ambitions, especially toward Taiwan; as Chinese Lieutenant-General Xiong Guangkai told U.S. diplomat Charles Freeman in a famous 1996 exchange, "You care more about Los Angeles than you do about Taipei."[17] Investments in sea-based missile defenses would not only protect against the North Korean long-range ballistic-missile threat but also require the Chinese to reinvest heavily in their deterrent, diverting resources now allocated to accelerating their power-projection capabilities.

The Current and Future Force. Today's navy is, far more than the army, a reflection of Cold War force planning. In some sense, because of the decades-long operational life of ships—up to fifty years in the case of aircraft carriers—this is to be expected. Yet, even before the reorientation of U.S. military strategy that has followed the September 11, 2001, attacks and the invasions of Iraq and Afghanistan, serious questions were being raised about the future of the navy. In the late 1990s, Vice Admiral Arthur Cebrowski, then president of the Navy War College and commander of Naval Warfare Development Command, proposed that the fleet be reorganized as a network and that its focus shift from open-ocean warfare to littoral power projection.[18] To naval reformers such as Cebrowski, who went on to lead the Pentagon Office of Force Transformation during the first term of the Bush administration, "The power of the 21st century fleet would be measured less by the number of carrier battle groups and surface combatants in the total ship battle force and more by the combined sensing and combat power of the total force battle network."[19]

Thus, the navy's modernization plan, intended to continue carrier construction and a new fleet of 116 cruisers and destroyers, was simply an extension of late-twentieth-century sea-power theory, maximizing the combat power of each individual ship. The centerpiece of service research and future procurement plans was the DD-21, a more capable ship but essentially similar to the current Aegis radar–equipped, Arleigh Burke–class ships. Cebrowski's concept of a smaller "Streetfighter" ship intended to maximize the number of nodes in the naval network—and to sail in close to shore—found few supporters in the navy leadership of the late Clinton administration.

The Bush administration, pushing Defense Secretary Rumsfeld's version of force transformation, reversed course and enthusiastically embraced Cebrowski's small-ship concept; indeed, as head of the Office of Force Transformation, Cebrowski was the agent of change. What role the 9/11 attacks had in tipping the scales is impossible to say, but in November 2001 Admiral Vern Clark, chief of naval operations, announced that the DD-21 program was to morph into an entire new family of surface combatants, the large, multipurpose destroyer DD(X)—essentially a continuation of DD-21—an even larger CG(X) guided missile cruiser, and the new Littoral Combat Ship (LCS)—essentially, Cebrowski's "Streetfighter" come to life.[20] The LCS program has moved out at an extraordinarily rapid pace of development; two competing industry teams have been assigned the task of building two prototypes each by 2007 and then building as many as eighteen LCSs by 2011.

Nevertheless, it is difficult to avoid the conclusion that the navy may be doing some of the right things for all of the wrong reasons. Cebrowski's analyses are the product of pre-9/11 and certainly pre-Iraq thinking. The current vision of the navy is not so much of a force capable, at the "low end" of potential conflict, of policing littoral waters in the greater Middle East and elsewhere, while still fully able, at the "high end," of responding to a Chinese blue water challenge. The concept of the fleet as a network too often sounds like an end in itself. Bob Work of the Center for Strategic and Budgetary Assessments has captured the navy's thinking succinctly:

> The Navy is pursuing a new, more distributed fleet architecture to fit its new vision of scalable battle networks. In the final stages of the Cold War, the fleet operated 12 independent strike groups. In the 1990s—as precision weapons increased individual carrier and surface combatant strike power—the fleet could muster 19 strike groups. Now, by leveraging information, precision, and networking, the Navy plans to operate a total of 37 smaller strike groups, nearly doubling the maximum number of strike forces in the carrier era. These smaller task groupings will form the building blocks for flexibly assembled battle networks that can be scaled for the mission at hand.[21]

To be sure, this is a wonderful vision of the future navy, but, like much of the current "transformational" thinking, it is entirely self-referential: it is all about assembling the network, which is supposed to simply be scaled to whatever the mission might be. There is no reference to an actual enemy or even to a geopolitical or operational scenario wherein naval power is essential. And, most of all, striking power is assumed to be the primary measure of effectiveness. In littoral missions throughout the greater Middle East, this may be the least of the U.S. military's worries. The curious result is that the metric of "presence," used to justify the size of the navy and the number of carriers during the Cold War, may now be a more appropriate benchmark of maritime capabilities for many missions.

Conversely, under the conditions that are likely to be the case in a crisis involving China, the value of the LCS may be quite limited. The original critique of the "Streetfighter"—that it was too

vulnerable to a technologically sophisticated opponent—
still seems valid as the Chinese navy accelerates its own modernization program and raises the challenge of "access" not only to
the Taiwan Strait itself but also in the nearby open ocean. To be
sure, the navy would operate in a networked fashion in such a
scenario, but the need would be for highly robust "nodes." This
is the scenario in which large-ship strike groups would prove
their worth.

Submarines. The seemingly forgotten factor in U.S. Navy planning over the past decade has been the submarine force, particularly the attack submarine force. The Cold War was a very
submarine-intensive military competition, with ballistic-missile
boats eventually forming the most survivable leg of the nuclear
triad and the ever-expanding game of hide-and-seek with the
Soviet navy. The famous 600-ship fleet of the Reagan years was to
have fully 100 attack submarines.

The role of ballistic-missile submarines, dubbed "SSBNs" by
the navy, remains central to U.S. nuclear posture, albeit with a
reduced fleet. As noted earlier, four of these boats are being con-
verted to an "SSGN" configuration, substituting conventional
Tomahawk land-attack cruise missiles for their Trident nuclear
systems. This move is a reflection of the navy's new predilection
for projecting strike power ashore; each SSGN will be fitted to
carry as many as 154 Tomahawks. These massive boats are also
ideal for naval special warfare operations, particularly for insert-
ing SEAL teams. And future modifications of the SSGN may
include the ability to carry smaller unmanned underwater vehicles or other new systems.[22]

Thus, the bulk of the navy's submarine fleet is still nuclear-
powered attack submarines, or SSNs. Although previous defense
reviews have varied slightly in their appreciation of the attack
submarine requirements, most experts have generally thought
that a fleet of fifty-five to sixty-two attack boats was needed. An
internal Defense Department paper in 1999 recommended
increasing the size of the fleet to sixty-eight by 2015 and to

seventy-six by 2025.[23] In its 2001 QDR, the Bush administration returned to the older and smaller numbers.[24]

The uncertainty over the role of submarines in the post–Cold War force has been a reflection of the uncertainty of the mission. In the wake of the Soviet Union's demise, the submarine fleet seemed to have lost much of its *raison d'être*. But through the 1990s, the covert intelligence, surveillance, and reconnaissance capabilities of attack submarines came to be prized, although less so by the navy itself than by the White House and National Security Council. Attack submarines were, for example, considered for long-term snooping missions off the coast of South America as part of the antidrug interdiction campaigns. And as cruise-missile strikes became a central aspect of Clinton administration policies from the Balkans to Afghanistan, the worth of a very stealthy, long-loitering, highly accurate strike platform seemed to rise.

But the Bush administration was openly contemptuous of the Clinton "pin-prick" policy and has grown increasingly skeptical of using submarines for open-ended spying missions, particularly after September 11, when the nature of the intelligence target changed fundamentally. The administration has preferred investments in other intelligence platforms, from satellites to, increasingly, unmanned aerial vehicles. Perhaps more telling, the Pentagon seems to have growing doubts about the value of cruise missiles, perhaps in response to the proliferation of satellite-guided bombs. Thus, the recent "program budget decision" memorandum directs that the navy's submarine procurement be held at one boat per year, with the long-term result of reducing the fleet to perhaps thirty to thirty-five subs.[25]

Two Fleets in One. In sum, the U.S. Navy is really evolving toward two quite different kinds of fleets: a mostly littoral, brown water patrolling fleet to support U.S. strategy for the greater Middle East, and an open-ocean, high-technology, firepower-intensive blue water fleet for duty in the Indian Ocean and western Pacific. This is the classic posture of the "high-low mix," or "green water" fleet.

If anything, the shift toward such a posture should be accelerated. Naval "presence" missions in a post-Iraq environment are as valuable as they were during the Cold War—if not more so—but the requirement for, say, patrolling in the Gulf of Guinea against terrorists or pirates is fundamentally different from patrolling the famous "Greenland-Iceland-United Kingdom gap" against Soviet submarines. The Littoral Combat Ship, of marginal value as a strike platform, seems ideal for such missions; indeed, it is hard to distinguish it from the frigate-size vessel that is part of the Coast Guard's "Deepwater" program, and it might make sense to consider a variant of that vessel as an LCS candidate.

The crunch, for the navy, comes at the high end of the fleet mix. For several decades, since the introduction of Aegis-class destroyers, the U.S. Navy has essentially been entirely a high-end force; the mix of nuclear-powered carriers, missile cruisers, destroyers, and attack submarines is perhaps qualitatively the finest fleet in human history. But retaining a high-end fleet for every global mission is increasingly expensive and problematic: as each ship becomes more sophisticated and more capable, it must be more carefully deployed and employed.

As argued above, the primary role of the high-end navy is in the western Pacific and, more frequently in the future, in the Indian Ocean. This is not to argue that navy planning ought to be focused exclusively on these regions. However, it is crucial to recognize that traditional service planning, carefully balancing the Atlantic and Pacific fleets and including constant carrier deployments in the Mediterranean and the Persian Gulf, is anachronistic.

In rough terms, the U.S. Navy's high-end mix of carriers, cruisers, destroyers, and submarines needs to be a "one-and-one-half" war fleet, immediately ready for contingencies in the Pacific, imminently ready for contingencies elsewhere—such as the kind of "nuclear nightmare" scenarios described above—and, in such regions as the Middle East, regarded as a supplement to the land-based forces, who carry the bulk of the burdens. Given the incredible capabilities of today's fleet, it is probably appropriate to trim its size while continuing to modernize it at a somewhat slower rate and gradually concentrating its operations in the Pacific. A fleet of eight or nine aircraft carriers is probably sufficient, as is a surface fleet of about one hundred ships, the majority of which are multipurpose vessels similar to the Arleigh Burke–class ships, but with perhaps ten or fifteen cruisers optimized for ballistic-missile defense.

The greatest risk in the navy's current program and posture is the shrinking size of the submarine force. The newest Virginia-class boats are highly capable but, at $2 billion apiece, are double the cost of the previous generation Los Angeles–class attack submarines that form the backbone of today's fleet. The upcoming QDR needs to consider a number of alternatives. One possibility is to modify another pair of Trident ballistic-missile boats to the SSGN configuration, preserving SSNs for more traditional missions such as antisubmarine warfare, a role whose value will again rise as China's navy becomes more capable. Another alternative is to consider a high-low mix of submarines, reintroducing smaller, shorter-range diesel submarines into the U.S. Navy, both to expand the number of submarines readily available in the Pacific and Indian oceans and to conduct less-demanding missions associated with the global war on terrorism. What the LCS does for the future surface fleet, a new class of diesel boats could do for the submarine fleet.

The Air Force: Time for a Real Revolution

The revolution in airpower of the past several decades has achieved almost every goal anticipated by its original theorists. However, there are still only a few cases where U.S. airpower can be said to have "won" a war in the sense of being politically decisive. The atomic bombs dropped on Hiroshima and Nagasaki and the seventy-eight-day air campaign in Kosovo are only partial vindications, as Japan surrendered only after a four-year amphibious campaign rendered the homeland vulnerable to invasion, and the outcome of Kosovo was only barely decisive. The "shock and awe" attacks at the start of Operation Iraqi Freedom are more the rule: they were extremely powerful and made a huge contribution to the ultimate success of the invasion, but as we have seen, they were far from decisive.

Perhaps more genuinely revolutionary has been the vastly improved coordination between precise airpower and ground maneuver. In Afghanistan, the combination of U.S. special forces, Afghan militiamen, and American airpower scattered the Taliban and al Qaeda forces whenever they massed to defend a city or a vital point. Precision airpower has even changed the face of urban combat: in, for example, the Fallujah operations of this past fall, marines and soldiers maneuvered to fix insurgent forces in place and then, as often as not, relied on firepower from the air to destroy them.

This revolution in airpower is more properly understood as a revolution in precision strike. Before the introduction of precision-guided missiles and bombs, air strikes were accurate within approximately 500 feet; today's satellite-guided bombs are accurate to within 20 feet and laser-guided bombs to within 10 feet.[26] These exponential improvements in accuracy have truly transformed air force operations. In the invasion of Iraq, fully 68 percent of the bombs dropped were precision guided.[27] Almost certainly the proportion of precision weapons used during the counterinsurgency campaign is even higher.

However, this increasingly effective marriage of land maneuver forces with precision airpower rests on the almost unquestioned assumption of U.S. air supremacy. Since the end of the Cold War, U.S. air forces have had no serious or sustained contest over any air space on the planet. During the invasion of Iraq, the Iraqi air force did not fly a single sortie. Through Operation Desert Storm and the no-fly-zone operations of the following decade, the Balkans wars, or Operation Iraqi Freedom, land-based air defenses have had almost no significant effect on U.S. air operations.

A final component in the advance in airpower has been the revolution in airborne reconnaissance, surveillance, intelligence gathering, and battle management capabilities. From large, specially designed aircraft such as the Airborne Warning and Control System (AWACS) and Joint Surveillance and Target Attack Radar System (JSTARS) to the proliferation of various electronic "pods" on tactical aircraft, the ability to find an enemy and target him rapidly and from great distance has grown by leaps and bounds.

In sum, U.S. military forces are addicted to these amazing airpower capabilities. Yet, like the rest of the armed services, today's air force is essentially an improved but smaller version of its Cold War self. The question before the 2005 Quadrennial Defense Review is how to shape the air force to meet the largely unanticipated and increasingly challenging missions described above. It is far from clear that today's air force is suited to the nation's new needs.

Air Cavalry. Previous defense reviews have been very kind to airpower generally and to the air force in particular. Through multiple reviews the air force has preserved its essential force structure and program goals, especially in regard to tactical aircraft. To be sure, reductions have been made in the bomber and ballistic-missile fleets. The curious result is a force increasingly dominated by shorter-range aircraft even as the service itself has begun to acknowledge its truly global missions.

Today's force is well suited to the missions in the greater Middle East in large part because the long-term commitment of the Bush administration to the region goes a long way to ensuring that American airpower will have continuing access to the region. Indeed, since 9/11 the variety and span of facilities used by U.S. aircraft have been quite stunning, ranging from Central Asia to West Africa to Southeast Asia. Prior to 9/11, the emerging concern of U.S. military planners was the question of access to the region; given anything near the current level of American military presence in the future, the value of a tactical air force in Middle East operations will continue to be far higher than imagined in the 2001 QDR.

But if that is the good news, the bad news is that as these kinds of operations endure—call them air cavalry missions—at such high levels, the legacy fleets of F-15s and F-16s are being ridden into premature old age. Just as the Defense Department needs to adjust its thinking about army and navy structures to deal with the nature of the long-term mission in the greater Middle East, so does the air force. A number of solutions are possible, from continued production of F-16s to the creation of a fleet of long-loitering unmanned aerial vehicles designed as on-call fire support for ground maneuver forces. One of the measures of the upcoming QDR is how well it addresses this issue.

There are also many reasons to adopt a "high-low mix" philosophy for the air force, analogous to the navy approach suggested above. Operations in the greater Middle East are likely to have a relatively low air-defense threat for the immediate future.

The High End. The likely airpower requirements of the two other scenarios discussed above demand far different and more highly sophisticated kinds of aircraft. A crisis over the Taiwan Strait or a nuclear "nightmare" in Pakistan, for example, might be beyond the capabilities of the current or planned air force.

The most immediate challenge in such operations, no matter the precise tactics imagined, is how to conquer the tyranny of distance. Although the navy would play a central role in any East Asian crisis, the United States would also have to rely on land-based air force aircraft. Although the B-2 bomber would be a key platform, and the air force is improving its facilities on Guam to handle B-2 operations and maintain its stealthy systems, the B-2 fleet comprises just sixteen airplanes.[28] Of course, with tanker support, F-117s and F-15 and F-16 tactical fighter bombers— and in future the F-22—could operate from Taiwan, Japan, and South Korea, for example. However, Taiwanese airfields are likely to be at risk (and, of course, political considerations have long prevented U.S. air forces from conducting training on Taiwan), and Japanese and Korean airfields are likewise within range of Chinese strikes. Allowing U.S. aircraft to operate from those countries would in fact make them part of the crisis or bring them directly into a conflict—a politically uncertain proposition at best.

A Taiwan Strait, Pakistan, or Iran crisis would occur in a far more dangerous air-defense environment than faced in recent years in Afghanistan, Iraq, or the Balkans. Moreover, whether there would be sufficient time for a methodical air-defense suppression campaign is unclear; the urgency of responding to a nuclear event or of reacting to provocative Chinese actions over the strait militates against excessive caution. Such scenarios make a stronger case for stealthy attack aircraft such as the F-22 and today's B-2s and F-117s, but none of these is ideal or sufficient. One way to make the most of the B-2 fleet—now that the production line is closed and cold—is to upgrade the electronics systems, particularly the outdated computer architecture. The bomber would also be much more flexible if it carried sensors and other systems to detect unanticipated air-defense radars and adjust its flight path accordingly.[29]

Nevertheless, the air force's plans for its "high-end mix" fleet need to be more thoroughly scrutinized in the 2005 QDR than in past reviews, and particularly in light of these emerging threat scenarios. In recent years, air force leaders have talked about a redesigned F-22 that would extend the Raptor's range and payload, but this idea promises to be a very expensive solution for what is perhaps marginal improvement. Perhaps more promising would be a large unmanned aerial vehicle, a kind of unmanned B-2.

The Other Air Force. Beyond these questions about the combat systems of the air force lie equally important decisions to be made about the service's support aircraft, most notably its fleets of tanker and cargo aircraft. Again, past defense reviews have tended to pay less attention to such issues, and so the service finds itself today with an insufficient fleet of C-17 airlifters and an increasingly decrepit fleet of tanker aircraft. Such systems are key to far-flung air operations; they put the "global" in U.S. airpower.

The initial decision to restrict the C-17 program was made in the early 1990s by then defense secretary Dick Cheney. Primarily a cost-cutting choice, it was nonetheless a reflection of how dimly understood the post–Cold War world was at the time. The plan then was to buy just 120 C-17s, but the revised program calls for another 60 planes. The problem is that airlift needs—that is, the reality of the operations of the recent past translated through a series of formal Pentagon "mobility studies"—are constantly expanding. Thus, the air force would like to buy another forty or so C-17s, extending the buy past 2020. Even if we allow that some formal airlift requirements may be based on very faulty reasoning about the need to move large ground units by air, the need for greater airlift capacity is real.

Equally crucial is the need to address the problem of aerial refueling. Unfortunately, the scandal surrounding the air force's plan to lease rather than purchase new tankers will exacerbate the problem by delaying any solution. Tanker aircraft have become increasingly essential to U.S. military operations; in Operation Iraqi Freedom, tanker aircraft flew more than 6,000 sorties, more than a quarter of the total air force sorties.[30] With future operational requirements driven by the need for greater range, the need for tankers is equally important, doubling or tripling the combat range of both tactical aircraft and long-range bombers as well as the range of cargo aircraft.

The current tanker fleet of KC-135 aircraft averages forty-four years of age. Even more than combat aircraft such as F-15s and F-16s, these tankers are reaching obsolescence and plagued by low readiness rates. The upcoming QDR must address the requirement to accelerate a tanker replacement program even as the various investigations surrounding the collapsed leasing program continue—even if that means initiating a competition between Boeing, the only American manufacturer capable of building a large tanker aircraft, and arch-rival Airbus, the European consortium.

Best and Worst of Times. Over the early years of the post–Cold War era and through the initial quadrennial defense reviews, the U.S. Air Force has enjoyed tremendous successes. The revolution in precision strike seemed to validate its airpower theories, and the branch was rewarded in Pentagon budget wars. This run of fortune continued through the invasion of Afghanistan and the hopes for a quick "shock and awe" victory over Saddam Hussein. But the long-term realities of the U.S. military engagement in the Middle East have brought the assumptions of airpower theory into question. Nuclear "nightmare" and East Asia scenarios undercut the rationale for the service's heavy investment in short-range tactical aircraft. Thus, the air force approaches the 2005 QDR with a sense of foreboding.

Conclusion: Defense Budgets

"No one had anticipated that the cost of Iraq would continue to grow like [this]."[1] Thus spake Dov Zakheim, until last year the Pentagon's comptroller and an original member of Defense Secretary Rumsfeld's brain trust, early in January when the press got its hands on the Pentagon's "program budget decision" for the 2006 defense budget.[2] It would be hard to find a more succinct expression of the dilemma the Defense Department now faces and why the crisis described in the first sentence of this report is so deep and immediate. The strategies, the missions, the military posture, and armed services described in the report are all unrealistic without significantly increased defense budgets. Conversely, without greater spending, the very structures of America's defenses—most particularly the U.S. Army—are in danger of precipitate collapse. The expansive Bush Doctrine is built on a dangerously fractured foundation.

Expressing the gap between strategic ends and military means in dollar terms is much more art than science, but a fair guess is about $100 billion per year. According to Steven Kosiak, a defense budget analyst at the Center for Strategic and Budgetary Assessments, the true cost of the current defense program—that is, if the current program were adequately funded—would be approximately $500 billion per year.[3] That number does not include the additional cost of operations in Iraq and Afghanistan, estimated by Zakheim now to be $7 billion per month, or about $1 billion per month more than in 2004.[4] The total "emergency" supplemental appropriation request for such operations in 2005 may well reach $100 billion.

81

One of the largest chunks—if not the single largest—of these additional defense costs is devoted to paying the salaries and benefits of Army National Guard personnel and reservists called to active duty. In other words, the costs of operations in Iraq have grown in an unanticipated way simply because the manpower requirements have so exceeded predictions. The puzzle is, at this point, why the Bush administration continues to act as if these personnel needs are merely temporary.

The most likely explanation is narrowly political: under government budget rules, supplemental appropriations do not count when calculating the federal deficit. With annual deficits at about $500 billion, the cry for governmental fiscal discipline has returned and with it an expectation that the Pentagon should contribute its "fair share" to cost-cutting efforts. Thus, the administration plans to cap baseline defense budgets at slightly more than $400 billion and hope that supplemental spending can relieve some of the pain.

Yet in an $11 trillion-plus American economy, this level of defense spending still represents less than 4 percent of gross domestic product. Indeed, by this measure, Bush baseline budgets have been barely more than late Clinton-era defense budgets. Even when the costs of Iraq and Afghanistan are added, total spending is less than 5 percent of gross domestic product, well below the Cold War average of 6 to 7 percent and far less than in peak Cold War years during the Vietnam or Korea conflicts.

Liberal and libertarian critics rightly point out that, in inflation-adjusted dollars, today's defense budgets rival those of the Reagan buildup. More revealing and relevant is the fact that the overall U.S. economy is half again as large as in the 1980s; Americans are simply much richer. Thus, the only consistent way to judge defense spending through the years—and certainly the best measure of our willingness to sacrifice—is as a proportion of our overall wealth.

Over time, the final reckoning of defense budgets has been: how much is enough? Current levels of military spending are clearly not enough. We have failed to create ground forces large enough to sustain our commitment in the Middle East. Having failed to predict that risk or to address it adequately, the administration is looking to weapons procurement to offset the costs—thus the program cuts recently outlined.[5] The idea, essentially, is to push the risk off in the hope that current systems—most of which were designed and built during the Reagan years or before—can be repaired and operated years longer than planned. Perhaps at some point in the next decade the process of defense transformation will have reached a level of maturity and critical mass sufficient to create entirely new forces.

But this approach does more to magnify the risk than to postpone it. As argued in this paper, the demands of current operations in the Middle East continue to exceed the administration's predictions. Rather than rebuilding U.S. ground forces, the administration is consuming them ever more rapidly. It risks simply breaking the professional army and conveniently ignores the continued role of the Marine Corps in Iraq.[6] The same is true of tactical air forces, which now carry a far larger burden of providing fire support to land maneuver forces. With regard to the sea, the administration has chosen to dangerously shrink the submarine fleet.

Budget shortfalls also endanger many of the Pentagon's most promising reform programs. The army's "modularity" initiative, designed to create an increased number of interchangeable, brigade-size "units of action," has been slowed because of personnel shortages. So has the initiative to realign the U.S. military posture in Europe. And the upcoming round of domestic base realignments and closures, which might save money in the longer term but will increase spending in the near term, could well be delayed or downsized for a combination of budgetary and political reasons.

In truth, we need only increase defense budgets by about 5 to 10 percent over the amount of money actually being spent now. The combination of the current baseline budget plus supplemental appropriations puts total defense spending at about $500 billion per year; that is close to being the right level of funding. The most immediate fiscal challenge for the Pentagon is to alter the way that money is spent. "How?" is as important a question as "How much?"

Relying so heavily on supplemental funding distorts the Defense Department's priorities and perverts proper planning. "Converting" perhaps half the "emergency" money into "normal" money, primarily for the purpose of expanding the army and Marine Corps, would address many of the problems of force sizing while reducing the pressure on the reserve components. It would not relieve National Guard personnel and Army Reservists from all participation in long-running constabulary operations, but it would reduce their responsibility to a more manageable level and restore them to their traditional role as a truly strategic reserve, as genuine citizen-soldiers. Nor would such a plan eliminate the need for supplemental funding, but it would reduce much of the uncertainty that now plagues the Pentagon. Ramping up the baseline budget by $30–40 billion over the next five years would allow army active end strength to grow to 625,000 and the Marine Corps to perhaps 210,000.

Equipment modernization requires nearly as much additional funding as military manpower. The Bush administration's idea of transformation has been premised on a period of rapid transition from today's force to the force of tomorrow.[7] The idea, enunciated by the president in the 2000 campaign, was to skip a generation of weaponry. Too little weight is given to the period of transition, when it is clear that U.S. forces will not be afforded a "strategic pause" to radically rearm and refit. Pentagon procurement decisions still reflect this view, from the cancellation of the army's Crusader howitzer and Comanche scout helicopter to the more recent program budget decisions on the air force's F-22 and other systems. Defense officials had hoped to "reset" the force for transformational purposes after the initial success in invading Iraq, rather than "recover" it by restoring it to its prewar status.

Weapons of the F-22 generation—late–Cold War designs and concepts—are quite obviously imperfect for the emerging missions of the twenty-first century. However, they form a crucial link between the upgraded Reagan-era force of today and the transformed force of tomorrow. Because of the unforeseen pace of operations since September 11, 2001, the legacy force is being worn down far faster than anticipated. Many production lines are already closed, and if planned administration cuts are made, more will close, such as the C-17 airlifter, before military requirements are close to being met.

The United States cannot afford a modernization program so heavily dependent on revolutionary transformation. Engaged as a global superpower in a set of missions that exhaust the current force, the Pentagon should content itself with evolutionary change and pay more attention to the period of transition. The newer systems just entering production are needed to cover this period—which will last a decade or more. Although it makes no sense to buy the full production of F-22 or the Joint Strike Fighter systems anticipated originally, neither does it make sense to so reduce these programs to the point of crippling the force in five or ten years.

Even ramping up modernization budgets by $40 billion per year would not fully fund the total defense program now on the books. Indeed, a number of the recent Pentagon program decisions, such as retiring older nonnuclear aircraft carriers, are smart moves. But the combination of increased spending for current operations and a shift in investment to potentially transformational systems has created a kind of parting of the budgetary waters that leaves near-term modernization programs high and dry. Recapitalizing the force is made only more risky by postponement.

Finally, the Pentagon needs to fund better its reposturing initiatives, ranging from the internal reorganization of the armed services to the relocation of forces to the Middle East and Southeast Asia and the realignment of facilities stateside. Little analytical work has been conducted to estimate the costs of such moves, but they will be expensive propositions requiring billions in up-front investment. Moreover, given the unpredictability of the world, there is no guarantee of long-term savings; the value of these initiatives is to be measured in improved capabilities and more effective operations.

In sum, the United States must expect to devote something like 5 percent of gross domestic product—a nickel on every dollar—to its defenses. To repeat, this is not much of an increase over current actual spending levels; most of the increases in the baseline budget would be offset by reductions in supplemental funding. Nor are defense budgets of such magnitude unprecedented or inconsistent with a growing economy. Most important, that level of spending just might be enough to sustain the force needed to underwrite a continued Pax Americana.

Notes

Introduction

1. Peter Slevin, "U.S. Promises Democracy in Middle East; Rice Calls for 'Generational Commitment,'" *Washington Post*, August 8, 2003, A01.

2. George W. Bush, *The National Security Strategy of the United States* (Washington, D.C.: White House, September 2002), available at www.whitehouse.gov/nsc/ nss.html.

3. The Bush Doctrine has meant different things to different people at different times. In March 2001, *Washington Post* columnist Charles Krauthammer defined the Bush Doctrine as a return to "the unabashed unilateralism of the 1980s," as exemplified by the administration's push for national missile defense, its rejection of the Kyoto Treaty, and its broader belief that the "U.S. can reshape, indeed remake, reality on its own." Within hours of the September 11 attacks, the Bush Doctrine was dramatically recast as the administration's pledge to make no distinction between terrorists and the states that sponsor them. In 2002, following the president's graduation speech at the U.S. Military Academy at West Point, the Bush Doctrine assumed another meaning, this time associated with the concept of preemption against threats to U.S. national security. With the publication of the *National Security Strategy* later that year, the term has become increasingly associated with the U.S. commitment to a "forward strategy of freedom" and President Bush's assertion, as he put it in his second inaugural address, that "the survival of liberty in our land increasingly depends on the success of liberty in other lands."

These shifts in the public understanding of the Bush Doctrine are entirely natural—a reflection of the Bush administration's own evolving thinking about American grand strategy in the post-9/11 world and the momentous events that have driven it. This is an evolution that will continue until January 2009 and possibly beyond, compelled as much by unforeseen developments in the world as anything that happens in the Oval Office. It is precisely for this reason that the term "Bush Doctrine" is taken by this paper in the widest possible sense to mean the strategic goals that the Bush administration has defined for the United States since the September 11 attacks: the transformation of the political order in the greater Middle East and the broader international order in ways that will advance, defend, and favor human freedom. (Charles Krauthammer, "The Bush Doctrine," *Time,* March 5, 2001, p. 41; George W. Bush, "President Bush Discusses Freedom in Iraq and Middle East," The White House, Office of the Press Secretary, November 6, 2003; George W. Bush, "Second Inaugural Address," The White House, Office of the Press Secretary, January 20, 2005.)

4. Michael Mandelbaum, "Foreign Policy as Social Work," *Foreign Affairs,* January/February 1996, p. 16.

5. Richard B. Myers, *National Military Strategy of the United States of America, 2004: A Strategy for Today; A Vision for Tomorrow* (Washington, D.C.: U.S. Department of Defense, 2004), 18.

6. Ibid., 18–19.

7. "Force transformation" is the Pentagon's term of art to describe the modernization of the U.S. military—a continuous process that encompasses changes in technology, personnel, institutions, and concepts, "meant to create or anticipate the future" in ways that ensure "sustained American competitive advantage in warfare." (Vice Admiral Arthur K. Cebrowski (Ret.), "What Is Transformation?" Office of Force Transformation, available at http://www.oft.osd.mil/.)

Chapter 1: Strategies

1. Thomas L. Friedman, "U.S. Vision of Foreign Policy Reversed," *New York Times,* September 22, 1993, A13.

2. White House, *A National Security Strategy for a New Century* (Washington, D.C.: White House, 1999), iii, available at http://www.dtic.mil/doctrine/jel/other_pubs/nssr99.pdf.

3. George W. Bush, *The National Security Strategy of the United States* (Washington, D.C.: White House, September 2002), 1, available at www.whitehouse.gov/nsc/nss.html.

4. Gareth Harding, "Analysis: Europe-America Defense Gap," UPI, January 10, 2005.

5. For a fuller discussion, see Thomas Donnelly, *Operation Iraqi Freedom: A Strategic Assessment* (Washington, D.C.: AEI Press, 2004).

6. Bush, *National Security Strategy,* 27, available at www.whitehouse. gov/nsc/nss.html.

7. George W. Bush, "President Bush Discusses Freedom in Iraq and Middle East," The White House, Office of the Press Secretary, November 6, 2003.

8. Dave Moniz and Tom Squitieri, "Defense Memo: A Grim Outlook," *USA Today,* October 22, 2003, 1A.

9. National Commission on Terrorist Attacks upon the United States, *The 9/11 Commission Report: Final Report of the National Commission on Terrorist Attacks upon the United States* (New York: Norton, 2004), 365–66.

10. Ibid., 366.

11. Ibid., 366–67.

12. Ibid., 367.

13. U.S. Department of Defense, *Annual Report on the Military Power of the People's Republic of China* (June 2000), available at www.defenselink. mil/news/Jun2000/china06222000.htm.

14. Ibid.

15. Ibid.

16. U.S. Department of Defense, *FY04 Report to Congress on PRC Military Power,* 10, available at www.defenselink.mil/pubs/d20040528PRC.pdf.

17. Ibid.

18. Ibid., 9.

19. Ibid.

20. Ibid., 11.

21. Ibid.

22. Ibid., 13.

23. United States–China Economic and Security Review Commission, *2004 Report to Congress* (Washington, D.C.: U.S. Government Printing Office, 2004), 151.

24. Ibid., 14.

25. See, for example, Fred von der Mehden, *China and Long-Range Asia Energy Security: An Analysis of the Political, Economic and Technological Factors Shaping Asian Energy Markets* (Houston, Tex.: James A. Baker III Institute for Public Policy, Rice University, April 1999), 4, available at http://www.rice.edu/energy/publications/docs/AsianEnergySecurity_ EnergyConflictContemporaryAsia.pdf.

26. United States–China Economic and Security Review Commission, *2004 Report to Congress,* 151.

27. Ibid., 158.

28. Ibid.

Chapter 2: Missions

1. Jeffrey Goldberg, "In the Party of God: Hezbollah Sets Up Operations in South America and the United States," *New Yorker,* October 28, 2002; and Anthony Faiola, "U.S. Terrorist Search Reaches Paraguay," *Washington Post,* October 13, 2001, A21.

2. Larry Rohter, "China Widens Economic Role in Latin America," *New York Times,* November 20, 2004, A1.

3. "Gov. Bush and Defense," *Washington Post,* September 26, 1999, p. B06.

Chapter 3: Posture

1. James Brooke, "Looking for Friendly Overseas Base, Pentagon Finds It Already Has One," *New York Times,* April 7, 2004, A17.

2. Judy Sarasohn, "Schwarzenegger Muscling against Base Closings," *Washington Post,* November 11, 2004, A35.

3. Frances Lussier, "Options for Changing the Army's Overseas Basing" (Congressional Budget Office, May 2004), available at www.cbo.gov/showdoc.cfm?index=5415&sequence=0.

Chapter 4: The Armed Services

1. See James Fallows, "Will Iran Be Next?" *Atlantic Monthly,* December 2004, available at http://www.theatlantic.com/doc/200412/ fallows.

2. Andrew F. Krepinevich, *Transforming the Legions: The Army and the Future of Land Warfare* (Washington, D.C.: Center for Strategic and Budgetary Assessments, 2004), 21, available at www.csbaonline.org/ 4Publications/Archive/R.20040114.Transforming_the_L/R.20040114. Transforming_the_L.pdf.

3. James Dubik, *The Army's "Twofer": The Dual Role of the Interim Force* (Washington, D.C.: Institute of Land Warfare, 2001), 2.

4. Krepinevich, *Transforming the Legions,* 20, available at www.csbaonline.org/4Publications/Archive/R.20040114.Transforming_ the_L/R.20040114.Transforming_the_L.pdf.

5. Donald H. Rumsfeld, *Quadrennial Defense Review Report* (Washington, D.C.: U.S. Department of Defense, September 30, 2001), available at http://www.defenselink.mil/pubs/qdr2001.pdf.

6. Paul Wolfowitz, "Department of Defense Budget Priorities for FY 03," House Budget Committee, 107th Congress, Washington, D.C., February 12, 2002.

7. Secretary Francis J. Harvey and General Peter J. Schoomaker, "A Statement on the Posture of the United States Army 2005," Presented to the Committees and Subcommittees of the United States Senate and House of Representatives, 109th Congress, Washington, D.C., February 6, 2005, available at http://www.house.gov/hasc/testimony/109thcongress/Readiness/03-03-05CodyArmy.pdf.

8. John F. Kerry, "Kerry's Acceptance Speech," *New York Times*, July 30, 2004, p. 6.

9. Michael O'Hanlon, "The Need to Increase the Size of the Deployable Army," *Parameters* 34 (Autumn 2004), available at http://carlisle-www.army.mil/usawc/Parameters/04autumn/ohanlon.htm.

10. Tom Bowman, "A Different Guard Role in Iraq War," *The Sun* (Baltimore), September 14, 2004, A1.

11. See Thomas Donnelly, Margaret Roth, and Caleb Baker, *Operation Just Cause: The Storming of Panama* (Lanham, Md.: Lexington Books, 1991).

12. See "Stryker Brigade Combat Team," GlobalSecurity.Org, available at www.globalsecurity.org/military/agency/army/brigade-ibct.htm.

13. U.S. Army Training and Doctrine Command, TRADOC Pamphlet 525-3-90/O&O, *The United States Army Objective Force—Operational and Organizational Plan for Maneuver Unit of Action* (Fort Monroe, Va.: TRADOC, July 22, 2002), 25.

14. Ibid., 36, 37.

15. House Committee on Armed Services, "Statement by Honorable Gordon R. England, Secretary of the Navy," February 12, 2004, available at http://www.globalsecurity.org/military/library/congress/2004_hr/040212-england.htm.

16. Ibid.

17. Aaron Friedberg, "Broken Engagement," *Weekly Standard*, February 24, 1997.

18. An excellent summary of these events is in Robert O. Work, "Small Combat Ships and the Future of the Navy," *Issues in Science and Technology* (Fall 2004): 60–66.

19. Ibid., 63.

20. Ibid.

21. Ibid., 64.

22. For a fuller discussion of navy submarine issues, see Ronald O'Rourke, "Navy Attack Submarine Force-level Goal and Procurement Rate: Background and Issues for Congress," Congressional Research Service, June 2, 2004.

23. See "Navy Point Paper," *Inside the Navy*, February 14, 2000.

24. Rumsfeld, *Report on the Quadrennial Defense Review*, 23, available at http://www.defenselink.mil/pubs/qdr2001.pdf.

25. U.S. Department of Defense, "PBD 753: Other Secretary of Defense Decisions," December 23, 2004, p. 5, available at www. marinecorpstimes.com/content/editorial/pdf/dn.pbd753.pdf.

26. Steven Kosiak, *Matching Resources with Requirements: Options for Modernizing the Air Force* (Washington, D.C.: Center for Strategic and Budgetary Assessments, August 2004), 52.

27. U.S. Central Command Air Forces, "Operation Iraqi Freedom—By the Numbers," April 20, 2003, 11, available at www.globalsecurity.org/military/library/report/2003/uscentaf_oif_report_30apr2003.pdf.

28. The total B-2 fleet actually comprises twenty-one aircraft, but just sixteen of these are "combat coded"; the remainder are retained for training and other purposes.

29. For a fuller discussion of potential B-2 upgrades, see Barry Watts, *Backgrounder: Moving Forward on Long-Range Strike* (Washington, D.C.: Center for Strategic and Budgetary Assessments, September 27, 2004), 16–18.

30. U.S. Central Command Air Forces, "Operation Iraqi Freedom—By the Numbers," April 20, 2003, 7–8, available at www.globalsecurity.org/military/library/report/2003/uscentaf_oif_report_30apr2003.pdf.

Conclusion: Defense Budgets

1. Jonathan Weisman and Renae Merle, "Pentagon Scales Back Arms Plans; Current Needs Outweigh Advances in Technology," *Washington Post,* January 5, 2005, A1.

2. U.S. Department of Defense, "PBD 753: Other Secretary of Defense Decisions," December 23, 2004, available at www.marinecorpstimes.com/content/editorial/pdf/dn.pbd753.pdf

3. Steven Kosiak, "Current Defense Budgets" (presentation, American Enterprise Institute, Washington, D.C., January 13, 2005).

4. Dov Zakheim, "Current Defense Budgets" (presentation, American Enterprise Institute, Washington, D.C., January 13, 2005).

5. See Weisman and Merle.

6. Dov Zakheim's recent presentation at AEI was indicative of administration thinking in this regard. He described the Marine Corps as a force designed to "hedge" against unforeseen contingencies in regions other than the Middle East despite the continued large commitment of

Marines in ongoing Iraq operations. At recent levels of deployment, the Marine Corps would be incapable of responding to a significant crisis—one demanding multiple Marine expeditionary units—without first withdrawing from Iraq.

7. For a fuller discussion of the need for transition, see Thomas Donnelly, *Rebuilding America's Defenses: Strategy, Forces and Resources for a New Century* (Washington, D.C.: Project for a New American Century, 2000), 11–13, 69–76.

About the Author

Thomas Donnelly is a resident fellow in defense and security policy studies at the American Enterprise Institute and a member of the U.S.-China Economic and Security Review Commission. He is the author of *Operation Iraqi Freedom: A Strategic Assessment; Operation Just Cause: The Storming of Panama;* and *Rebuilding America's Defenses: Strategy, Forces and Resources for a New Century.*